the phone addiction *workbook*

How to Identify Smartphone Dependency, Stop Compulsive Behavior and Develop a Healthy Relationship with Your Devices

Hilda Burke

Ulysses Press

Published in the United States by:
Ulysses Press
P.O. Box 3440
Berkeley, CA 94703
www.ulyssespress.com

ISBN: 978-1-61243-903-7
Library of Congress Catalog Number: 2018967982

Printed in Canada by Marquis Book Printing
10 9 8 7 6 5 4 3 2 1

Acquisitions editor: Bridget Thoreson
Managing editor: Claire Chun
Editor: Renee Rutledge
Proofreader: Lauren Harrison
Front cover design: Justin Shirley
Cover art: © GoodStudio/shutterstock.com
Interior design: Jake Flaherty
Interior art: page 96 © Norwayblue/shutterstock.com

Smartphone Compulsion Test on pages 21 and 134 reprinted with permission from Dr. David Greenfield, The Center for Internet and Technology Addiction

Distributed by Publishers Group West

To Madra

Contents

Introduction 1

    Can We Really Become Addicted to Our Phones? 2

    A Bit about Me 3

    Mission of This Book 5

    How to Use This Book 5

    Start Tracking Actual Usage 6

CHAPTER 1: Mobile for Good: Positive Ways That Smartphone Technology Has Changed the World 8

    Innovation 9

    Raising Consciousness 10

    Reaching Out for Support 11

    Bringing People Closer 11

    Net Neutrality 12

    Exercises 13

CHAPTER 2: Why Are We So Hooked On Our Phones? 19

    How Addicted Are You? 21

    Why Do We Become Addicted? 23

    Neuroplasticity and Your Habits 26

    Breaking Patterns 26

    Wait Training 27

    What Can We Learn from Cocaine-Addicted Lab Rats? 28

    Exercises 30

CHAPTER 3: The Corrosive Power of Being Always Available 34

Always Working but Not Always Productive 35
Debunking Work Myths. 36
Placing Our Relationships On Hold 38
When It Starts to Hit Home. 40
Exercises. 41

CHAPTER 4: Smarter Phones, Dumber Users: How Your Phone Might Be Changing the Way You Think 48

Four Smart Reasons to Switch Off Your Phone 50
Mind Wandering. 57
On Meditation. 59
Exercises. 61

CHAPTER 5: Tackling Boredom and Emotional Discomfort. 69

Boredom and Addiction 71
Suppressed Emotions and Addiction 75
Exercises. 79

CHAPTER 6: Procrastination: Why We Really Put Stuff Off!. 87

1. Distractibility. 88
2. Time to Complete 89
3. Self-Confidence 89
4. Task Value 90
Sneaking Up on Procrastination 93
The Snowball Effect 94
But Remember to Love Thy Procrastinating Self 95
Exercises. 97

CHAPTER 7: On Contentment 104

Healthy Body, Healthy Mind 105

No Comparison. 108

Be the Change You Want to See 110

Know Thyself. 112

Unlock Your Cage. 114

Exercises. 116

Conclusion. 125

Appendix 128

Recommended Reading and Resources 135

Acknowledgments. 137

About the Author 138

Introduction

Paddington Station, if you've never passed through it, is a beautiful old station to the west of central London. Built in 1838, it was frequently bombed during World War II. Many troops passed through the station en route to the battlefields of Europe and beyond, and London children were evacuated from here during that same war. Its most famous "son" is undoubtedly he who bears (pun intended) the station's name—Paddington Bear. Four Tube lines pass through it as do many trains journeying west of England and beyond. Being an Irish native, I often take a Paddington train home, connecting to a ferry from Wales to Rosslare, a port on the east coast of Ireland. With a high-speed rail link to Heathrow Airport, Paddington Station also serves as a jumping-off point for many global travelers.

As you'd imagine, at such a cosmopolitan confluence point, the people-watching at Paddington is exquisite. Recently, I arrived there with a luxurious 45 minutes to spare ahead of my train's departure. I sat down and looked around and above me, taking in the beautiful vaulted roof, the stately old clock. Fifty years ago it probably didn't look much different. I imagined winding that beautiful clock back several decades and wondered what the people around me would have been doing then. Tourists would have wandered around taking pictures, someone would be checking the horse-racing results in a newspaper, another studiously poring over the stocks and shares. I imagined attractive strangers mingling glances, someone admiring their reflection in a pocket mirror, another surreptitiously biting their nails, a couple arguing.

Bringing my attention back to IRL (in real life) on a summer's day well into the twenty-first century, I gazed around at my contemporaries, and most people (old, young, black, white, male, female)—let's say at least 80 percent of them—were looking down intently at their phones. However, what they were doing on those devices was likely not dissimilar to what engaged their forebears of half a century ago. Perhaps some of them were even there 50 years ago doing the same thing but in a different way! As it states in Ecclesiastes: "The thing that hath been, it is that which shall be; and that which is done is that which shall be done: and there is no new thing under the sun."

Everything we can do on our smartphone, we could do previously in another way offline. But we now have Tinder or Grindr to check out attractive strangers, Instagram to see who's admiring us, a multitude of apps and news sites to update us on how our horse/investment is doing, and WhatsApp to spar or flirt remotely with our partner.

It's interesting how smartphones have been scapegoated for all society's ills when most of the behaviors they enable have been around for millennia—mating, narcissism, commerce, envy, lust. The difference now is availability and access. Take mating, or the pursuit of mating, for instance. In a primitive society our potential for partners was limited by geography. Now, with Tinder and its ilk we can set our conquest visions globally.

There has been an enormous pushback on tech corporations of late, and with good reason. They have invested billions in R&D to make their devices and apps stickier, more addictive, so that many of us cannot bear to be without them. However, blaming the tech companies for how we choose to spend our time and lying in wait for them to introduce modifications to render their offerings less attractive detracts from our own responsibility. Two vital weapons make up our arsenal against becoming slaves to our phones: freedom of choice and the ability to change. These two weapons, or "defense tactics," form the cornerstones of this book.

Can We Really Become Addicted to Our Phones?

The first step in tackling any issue is admitting it is an issue. This is a huge step because it involves humility and taking responsibility. Congratulations, because you've taken that first step. Even if you haven't purchased this book yourself, you've shown enough curiosity to read it to this point. You've also recognized that you need some help in making changes. Whether or not you find this book useful, possessing those two qualities alone is empowering.

The word "addiction" is so commonly used these days that it's lost some of its gravity. *Psychology Today* defines addiction as "engaging in the use of a substance or in a behavior for which rewarding effects provide incentive to repeatedly pursue the behavior despite detrimental consequences." Of course, there is some ambiguity here. What one person deems "detrimental" may differ from what another does; in other words, "to each their own poison." Most articles focusing on the perils of high smartphone usage inevitably label it "addiction," and any methods of coping or managing it are tagged as "detox." This mirrors society's polarized, all-or-nothing mentality. However, no matter how much we read or hear regarding what it's doing to our brains, bodies, relationships, work, play, communities, kids, and environment, it's only when we see the impact a high level of smartphone dependency has on our own lives at a personal level that we feel compelled to do something.

It's worth noting, however, that whether heavy, even obsessive, use of smartphones can be properly classified as an addiction is still up for debate. As a relatively new type of behavior, smartphone use is not easily categorized by the standard classifications of impulse disorders provided by the *Diagnostic and Statistical Manual of Mental Disorders, Fifth Edition* (*DSM-5*). The manual draws a clear line between behavioral addictions and substance addictions. While video games, exercise, food, shopping, work, and the internet in general (and online sex and gambling in particular) have all shown propensity for addictive behavior, only online gambling has been classified as an addiction according to the *DSM-5*.

I will, however, refer to "phone addiction" to describe a heavy level of phone dependency throughout this book, but bear in mind that some would categorize it as an impulse control disorder rather than an addictive disorder. Although the jury is still out, my feeling is you're reading this book because you feel your phone cannibalizes some of the time you'd like to spend on other activities, that it's impacting your emotional well-being and/or your relationships and those are certainly some of the hallmarks of an addiction.

A Bit about Me

I'm a natural fidgeter. I was, and remain, easily distracted. I went to school in pre-internet times and managed to find plenty of distractions without the assistance of a smartphone.

In the evenings, I'd spend hours on the phone with my friends (after spending seven hours with them already) until my parents shouted for me to get off it.

I'm writing this book as someone who feels the lure of distraction, who loves nothing better than veering off course. But I also bring my experience as a psychotherapist, couples counselor, and life coach, who witnesses again and again how phones impact my clients' lives in unhealthy ways. Mothers who admit to feeling guilty about being distracted on their phones when their kids want to play with them, couples who admit that sex (and in some cases, sleep) has taken second place since devices entered the bedroom, employees who struggle to stop responding to emails in the middle of the night because their bosses have grown so used to their responsiveness that they fear what might happen if they stopped. It's a huge issue.

Before embarking upon writing this book I wouldn't have said I was a phone addict, but I definitely used my phone too much. It was the first thing I reached for in the morning and the last at night, and I checked it incessantly during the day. It started to bother me, so I began to schedule "phone-free zones" for myself during the day. I also had my first insight into what liberation from my phone felt like during a five-day trek in the Colombian rainforest last year, which was literally off grid. Despite this trek being extremely physically strenuous (with 5 a.m. starts and 10-hour treks every day), I felt extremely rejuvenated at the end. Although my body was challenged, my brain had a total break. There were no Trump or Brexit updates, no client queries, no friend or family dilemmas to deal with.

The week before I finally put pen to paper on this book, the topic of phone addiction came up in a religious sermon, a panel discussion on the future of beauty, and several client sessions (in one, it was named as the final trigger to break up a two-year relationship)—and that was just IRL! Online, I came across at least a dozen articles and tweets on the topic. It's definitely in the zeitgeist.

A Zen quote I often share with my clients springs to mind: "In the beginner's mind there are many possibilities, in the expert's there are few." I'm still learning and observing more about my digital behavior. My clients, in particular, have taught me much from their stories of the impact that their devices have on their well-being, their relationships, and their work.

Today, I am more conscious of how I use my phone and more curious about what possibilities open up when I use my phone less.

Mission of This Book

At a recent talk on smartphone addiction, the speaker concluded by saying, "Your time is precious. Don't spend it on mindless browsing." It was a stark wake-up call, one that left many of us reflecting on how much time we frittered away online on a daily basis. If there's one thing I'd like to impart to you, dear reader, it is to realize that YOUR time is precious. You have but one life.

How often do we lose track of where the last 10, 30, or 60 minutes have gone? Often, they've ebbed away through scrambles down the rabbit holes of Google or Instagram as we leapfrog from one hyperlink or one follower to the next, debating whether to like or love a former school friend's baby. Meanwhile, the dog gets fatter, we stay in jobs we dislike for months, maybe years longer than we intend to, and our paintbrushes get drier. Many, many things get sidelined to the "I'd do X if only I had more time" category while seconds and minutes go astray as we scroll, click, and swipe.

It can sometimes feel that life is literally at our fingertips, lived through the medium of our phones. My wish is that as you reclaim your fingertips from your phone, it will allow more space for those activities that you wish you could do "if only you had more time."

I've written this book as if you were a client who came to me looking to address your phone dependency. I treat any presenting issue with curiosity, as usually, the "one thing" that the client first presents is but the symptom of their real issue. And so it is with phone dependency. For most users it's simply a Band-Aid, a coping mechanism to avoid dealing with something deeper. My goal in writing this book is to get underneath the skin of your phone use, to see what's really driving you to spend so much of your precious, limited time on your phone. My hope is that as you get to know yourself better, you can identify the triggers that lead you to spending too much time on your phone, ultimately helping you to develop a healthier relationship with your device.

How to Use This Book

There are seven working chapters in this book. Each chapter shares some of my thinking and experience on different aspects of phone use. Not all of them are negative, by the way.

Chapter 1, for example, looks at ways our phones, when used mindfully, can improve not just our own lives but society at large as well.

At the end of each chapter are exercises based on what that chapter has addressed. I've used all the exercises I suggest in this book myself or have worked with clients who have tried them. So, they're tried and tested as helpful in the quest to curb smartphone dependency.

The Phone Usage Pattern (PUP) chart is a log included at the end of the following seven chapters for you to monitor how your usage pattern changes. Seven weeks is roughly the halfway point between two conflicting estimates of the length of time needed to change a habit—21 or 66 days[1]—depending on who or what theory you're referring to. Either way, I believe it to be a sufficient time to try out different things and start to have a good feel for what works for you. If you find it's taking you longer to attain your goal, that's okay! I have included some spare PUP charts in the Appendix section at the end of the book for you to log your progress past the seven-week point, should you wish to.

I recommend reading a chapter per week, letting the stories and ideas percolate, and allocating at least an hour for the exercises, some of which will require quiet time and reflection. It also reads best chronologically as the later chapters build on what's come before.

Start Tracking Actual Usage

If you have an iPhone or iPad, Apple's new operating system incorporates usage tracking features "to help customers understand and take control of the time they spend interacting with their iOS devices." This functionality can be found in the settings folder as "Screen Time" and needs to be switched on as the default setting is off. Essentially there are three categories—entertainment, productivity, and social networking. Screen Time gives quite detailed information not only on usage and time spent on each of the categories above (along with breakdown of app usage within those three categories) but also what notifications you're most likely to pick up for (which I think is a really interesting insight). If you use several Apple devices it allows you to set limits across all your devices, not only your phone, which some might find a useful function.

---

1   Gretchen Rubin, "Stop Expecting to Change Your Habit in 21 Days," *Psychology Today,* October 21, 2009, https://www .psychologytoday.com/gb/blog/the-happiness-project/200910/stop-expecting-change-your-habit-in-21-days.

Google announced a beta version of Digital Wellbeing app in 2018, which looks like it offers a similar type of functionality as Screen Time. But at the time of writing, I couldn't see this on offer in the Google store for Android phone users. Google does, however, offer this app as a native one—like Screen Time—on Google phones, such as Pixel.

If you have a non-Google Android device, I urge you to download a phone usage monitoring app. Some will likely be outdated by the time you read this book. But currently, I'm finding Social Fever pretty useful and easy to use. It has a strong emphasis on what you'd rather be doing offline, which for me is the whole point! Other monitoring apps include Forest, MyAddictometer, and QualityTime, to name a few. I'd encourage you to experiment with a few, see what works best for you, and then stick with it.

CHAPTER 1

Mobile for Good: Positive Ways That Smartphone Technology Has Changed the World

"Whether technology's effect is good or bad depends on the user. It's important that we shouldn't be slaves to technology; it should help us."

—14th Dalai Lama

In the interest of full disclosure, I should state that before training as a psychotherapist, I worked in the telecom industry. Initially, I held a communications role for Orange, a mobile network operator, and then for the GSMA, a trade body that represents the interests of mobile operators worldwide. It's in my blood—my grandfather, Paddy Burke, worked on radio transmissions for the first transatlantic cable between Europe and the US, which laid the foundations for high-speed internet communications.

The telecommunications roles I performed were considerably more prosaic. In 2008, when I started working for Orange, the iPhone was shiny and new and the future looked very bright for the mobile telecom industry. Some of the projects I worked on still inspire me. One example is Orange's birth registration campaign. In Western and Sub-Saharan Africa, birth registration stands at less than half of all children born. To access education or health care services in these countries you need to have a birth certificate, but due to lack of the necessary paperwork many are denied these basic services. The journey to register a birth—up to two days' travel—is just not feasible for a lot of people due to cost or an inability to take time off from work or childcare. Orange worked with Uganda Telecom to design a basic mobile app that could be used by local village chiefs to record births in their communities. It was an overwhelming success. In Uganda, birth registrations in the pilot area stood at 12 percent before launch of the app, but following its uptake, 80 percent of births were being registered.

In Mozambique, mobile is being used in the fight against HIV and AIDS. British nonprofit organization Absolute Return for Kids (ARK) incorporated mobile messaging to remind patients enrolled in antiretroviral therapy about appointment dates and to take their medication. Mobile reminders made a significant impact on compliance rates: 96 percent of users were still on track with their therapy after six months and 85 percent after 12 months, compared to a national average of 72 percent.

It's clear that smartphone technology is not all bad, far from it! It's important to recognize how phones can be used "smartly." Harnessed properly, our phones can be agents of social change, spreading awareness for important causes that otherwise may not gain traction and helping to bring together people who are geographically or socially separated. Our devices are not to blame for all society's ills. We do have a choice in how we use them. In this chapter, my aim is to bring some balance to the phone debate and shed light on how some people are harnessing mobile technology's capabilities to bring about positive change in their own and others' lives.

Innovation

Many developing countries have leapfrogged landline installation completely, adopting mobile on a broad scale due to the relatively low associated infrastructure costs. Nearly two-thirds of American households have landlines, while only 2 percent of African households do. This has fueled innovation and entrepreneurship in developing countries, with many third-world countries outstripping what we've achieved in the West.

Take Kenya's M-Pesa service, for instance, which lets users transfer money via text message. M-Pesa launched in Kenya in 2007, with similar systems launched by other telecom operators in Sub-Saharan Africa soon after. According to the Pew Research Center,[2] in 2014, 61 percent of Kenyans with cell phones reported making or receiving payments on their cell phones in the previous year, as did 42 percent of Ugandans and 39 percent of Tanzanians. Similar figures on mobile payments weren't available for the US that year, but according to Pew Research Center,[3] only 35 percent of US cell phone users were doing any form of mobile banking at that point. The World Bank estimates that the number of unbanked people dropped by 20 percent between 2011 and 2014,[4] which is largely attributed to mobile banking. The implications of this are massive. When people have access to basic banking services, it enables them to take micro loans, save, get financing, and invest for their future.

Raising Consciousness

Social media via mobile offers the potential for not-for-profit campaigns to reach a previously unimaginable global audience. One great example of this is the #Take3fortheSea campaign, encouraging people to take three pieces of litter away with them every time they visit the beach. How long would something like that have taken to gain traction offline? It's hard to imagine another way such a simple, important message would have been disseminated so consistently on a global basis.

Reflecting on my own personal mobile use, I remembered one occasion (before I started writing this book) waiting in line at the bank, when I was killing time by scrolling idly through my Facebook feed. Up popped a post by a charity I follow, with an urgent appeal to raise money for a particular initiative they needed support with. I had time to read it, and I felt moved. I clicked through and donated a small sum of money. The charity exceeded its target in a very short space of time that day, and I wondered how many others had made their donation in a similar way via their phones that day.

---

2   Jacob Poushter, "Which Developing Nation Leads on Mobile Payments? Kenya," *Pew Research Center,* February 18, 2014, http://pewrsr.ch/1gdOlE5.

3   Poushter, "Which Developing Nation Leads on Mobile Payments? Kenya."

4   The World Bank, "Massive Drop in Number of Unbanked, says New Report," April 15, 2015, http://www.worldbank.org/en/news/press-release/2015/04/15/massive-drop-in-number-of-unbanked-says-new-report.

Reaching Out for Support

My work as a psychotherapist is changing too with the advent of smartphone ubiquity. I sometimes conduct sessions via Skype, FaceTime, or WhatsApp video calls with clients who are working overseas. While holding a session through the medium of a mobile or tablet screen is definitely not the same as being in the same room together, it helps maintain the momentum of the work.

There are certainly clear benefits to online access to basic counseling services. I used to volunteer as a befriender for Samaritans, a UK- and Ireland-based charity providing emotional support to people who are in distress or at risk of suicide. Around 15 years ago, the organization started offering text-based befriending. There was huge resistance to it internally as many were cynical about what sort of "befriending" could be done within an SMS message of a 160-character maximum length. However, this basic service lowered the entry bar for many who wouldn't have considered reaching out for help otherwise, particularly those under 18. Thus, Samaritans managed to reach another target group of vulnerable young adults. In some cases, it was literally a lifesaver.

Online therapy appears to be growing in popularity, particularly in the US and the UK. In the UK, the doctor app Babylon offers therapy to 150,000 active users, while PlusGuidance, an online counseling service, has 10,000 users. Talkspace, a US-based online therapy platform, reports it has 500,000 registered users worldwide, with most in the US.

Bringing People Closer

The detrimental impact of mobile phones on relationships is well documented, and indeed it's something that rears its head frequently in my work with couples, which I'll address further in Chapter 3. However, there are instances where mobile telecommunications have served to provide a vital point of contact between families, friends, and partners who are separated geographically.

A particularly poignant case in point relates to a friend of mine. She and her partner met and dated in Singapore for a year before she moved back to London for work. Over the next two-and-a-half years they maintained their relationship long distance, only meeting every three to six months but seeing and speaking to each other every day via Skype. They even managed to have movie dates together using a mobile app called Let's Gaze. This wasn't a virtual relationship. It was a relationship that had been developed in real life and clearly had a strong foundation with both of them sufficiently invested in it for it to endure several years living apart on different continents. However, I wonder whether without advanced mobile technology it could have endured so successfully?

Net Neutrality

It's worth remembering that in and of themselves, our phones are neutral tools. It's what we do with them, what we download on them, and what we search for through them that has the capacity to help or hinder. As the Dalai Lama said, "Whether technology's effect is good or bad depends on the user."

A few years back, the supermodel Natalia Vodianova became frustrated with the futility and emptiness of the culture of "liking" on social media. However, she also took stock of her own power to garner these very likes. Rather than get stuck in a place of bemoaning how vacuous social media is or how fickle people can be, Vodianova decided to harness her influencer power for good.

In 2015, Vodianova, together with business partner and cocreator Timon Afinsky, launched Elbi, an app that simplifies charitable donations for smartphone users. Elbi focuses on giving a platform to smaller charities that users might not have heard of before.

As Vodianova commented upon Elbi's launch: "On social media, it has been ingrained within us to 'like' posts, as shared by our network, as a form of acknowledgment, acceptance, and resonance. It's the same principle on Elbi. We encourage users to 'love,' which is stronger than 'like,' because with each tap of the Love Button you are easily and securely donating $1 toward a meaningful cause."[5]

Is your mobile phone a help or a hindrance? The exercises that follow are designed to get you started with keeping track of how exactly you're spending your time on your device. Becoming aware of the most addictive but least beneficial apps or features is the first step toward changing your relationship with your device.

---

5   PR Newswire, "Elbi Turns Social Media Likes and Loves into Charitable Giving with Apple Pay," January 22, 2018, https://www .prnewswire.com/news-releases/elbi-turns-social-media-likes-and-loves-into-charitable-giving-with-apple-pay-300585659.html.

············· **EXERCISES** ·············

Phone Usage Patterns (PUP)   **Week 1**

	Mon	Tue	Wed	Thu	Fri	Sat	Sun
Total estimated time							
Messaging, texting							
Calls							
Browsing							
Shopping							
Dating							
Facebook							
Instagram							
Twitter							
Porn							
Netflix, Amazon Prime, YouTube							
Gaming							
Other							

What were the feelings that came up today?

Monday:

_____

_____

Tuesday:

_____

_____

Wednesday:

_____

_____

Thursday:

_____

_____

Friday:

_____

_____

Saturday:

_____

_____

Sunday:

_____

_____

How much time do you think you spent on your phone this week? Using the Phone Usage Patterns (PUP) chart starting on page 13, fill in your daily estimate in the box. Now do a rough breakdown of that time. Did you spend the most time on streaming videos? Texting? Dating apps? The monitoring app should help with this logging, but obviously, "web browsing" might include a lot of very different activities.

In the space provided above, note how you felt each day.

I'll be including this PUP chart and check-in questions at the end of each chapter, including how you try to curtail your phone use, and how effective that is from 0 (totally useless, had no effect) to 10 (totally effective) in reducing your phone usage. The goal here is to ascertain what triggers your phone dependency and what helps to reduce it. For some, it may be boredom, for others anxiety or sadness. By tracking your mood as well as your use, hopefully you can start to gain some insight into what it is you're trying to avoid or suppress by being on your phone. Also, by logging what tactics you're using to reduce your usage, you can hopefully start to notice what works for you.

Different things work for different people. I always remind my clients of this when they ask me for tips on how to deal with anxiety, sleeplessness, OCD, and the list goes on. If there was one approach that worked for everyone there'd be one diet book, one exercise book, and one stop-smoking book on the market! Try to break it down as honestly as you can, and be specific.

* * *

1. What did you try to reduce your phone use this week? Detail it here and rate its effectiveness on a scale of 0 to 10 (0 is totally useless, had no effect; 10 is totally effective).

_____

_____

_____

_____

_____

2. Write down what you'd like your phone usage to be—your final target.

Current use: _____ hours   Target use: _____ hours

Consider your final target and imagine that's where you're now at, that you've achieved your goal. Close your eyes and really visualize yourself only using your phone that amount per day. How would you like to use the time saved? Imagine, for instance, you have an extra hour in your day. How would you like to spend it?

_____

_____

_____

3. Ascertain precisely what you find so addictive on your phone.

What are you mainly using your phone for (the PUP chart on page 13 should help guide you on this!)?

_____

_____

_____

Thinking about this activity, if it were a food, what would it be? Would what you're consuming on your phone be nourishing—things to inspire, learn from, create with? Or are you ingesting junk food—stuff that feels good momentarily but ultimately leaves you feeling empty and craving more?

What would your phone content be if it were a food stuff?

_____

_____

_____

4. Create an inspiring lock screen.

The average smartphone user now checks their device, on average, every 12 minutes of the waking day. If you're reading this book, it's highly likely you're checking your phone even more frequently than this. Use this to your advantage!

Look at your response to question 2. Find an image that represents whatever you visualized doing with your time saved. It could be an old picture of yourself doing that very thing or a picture pulled from a magazine, a word, or even a little doodle. Just find something that strongly links you to that activity. It might be walking your dog more, having more face-to-face chats with your friends, or even sleeping!

My chosen word/image is: _____

Make it your phone lock screen. Every time you look at your phone, it'll be a reminder of what you really want to be doing with your time. I have a picture of my dog because a priority for me is spending more time with him when I'm not at work or writing my book. Visual cues are extremely powerful, especially when we're exposed to them over and over again. Imagine how much an advertiser would pay to have their products/services promoted on our home screen to us with such regularity!

5. Spring clean your phone.

Declutter your phone, getting rid of the apps that you no longer use or no longer serve you. Consider it as you would a packed closet—if it's overloaded with stuff, with many things hanging from the same hanger, it's impossible to see what you have, what you like, and what you no longer wear. I operate a one in, one out policy when I buy clothes, and I've found this also works well for apps. For most of us, our phone reflects ourselves; it's our mental real estate. Be particularly wary of mind-numbing apps such as Candy Crush, 2048, and card game apps. Gaming can be addictive and time consuming. Take some time to spring clean the following from your phone:

❏ **Shopping apps:** Reduce impulse shopping and reclaim time! Online shopping is easy to delete, and you can always do this from a computer if you really need something.

❏ **Food delivery (Uber Eats, Grubhub, Caviar, Seamless, Deliveroo):** Do you need to have this on your phone? Or could you just have this on your computer?

❏ **Social media (Twitter, Facebook, Instagram):** Consider deleting just one to start! Look at your usage as tracked in the Phone Usage Patterns chart. What can you do without?

List the mind-numbing apps that you use to kill time:

_____

_____

_____

_____

_____

_____

_____

_____

CHAPTER 2

Why Are We So Hooked On Our Phones?

"There are only two industries that call their customers 'users': illegal drugs and software."

—Edward Tufte

For many of us, a massage is the ultimate treat, a way to switch off and unwind while our physical and emotional stresses and strains are gently eased away by a skilled therapist. However, it seems many of us no longer want to switch off—at least, not our device.

I recently attended a beauty panel featuring renowned facialist, Nichola Joss (www .nicholajoss.com), who counts Margot Robbie, Elle Macpherson, Kate Moss, and Gisele Bündchen among the many A-listers in her client base. Joss explained that during a training session she ran recently, massage therapists expressed that their biggest dilemma was decoupling their clients from their devices before treatment. When I spoke to Joss afterward, she explained: "Touch therapy is one of the most significant things we can do in a treatment room for the well-being of a client to rebalance their energy, remove tension and stress. One of the main struggles is getting the client into a space of being fully in the present. Devices, phones, iPods, iPads—these all block us from being in the here and now. I always explain to my clients about the importance of disconnecting to help achieve a full sense of well-being and to optimize results from massage and facial treatments. One of the easiest ways to do this is to encourage our clients to mute their device and sit it away from the bed so as to not block any energy or give any distraction."

If we cannot bear to be separated from our smartphones for a 50-minute relaxation treatment, it's clear that we have an extremely dysfunctional relationship with our devices.

According to a 2016 report by Dscout,[6] the typical cell phone user touches his or her phone 2,617 times every day. A 2017 poll on mobile device usage from Common Sense Media revealed that 50 percent of US teens admitted that they "feel addicted" to their mobile devices. Phone users will sometimes put their lives in jeopardy to get their smartphone "hit"—according to research conducted by the National Safety Council (a nonprofit, public service organization promoting health and safety in the US), cell phone use was responsible for a quarter of reported car accidents in 2014.[7] The organization commented that the real figure is probably higher as most drivers will not voluntarily admit to using their devices while driving.

In the UK, an extensive 2017 Deloitte study of 4,150 16- to 75-year-old smartphone users found that 34 percent of those surveyed check their phone within five minutes of waking and a further 55 percent succumb to the lure of their device within 25 minutes of waking. Sixty-six percent of users check their phone during the night and 28 percent of 16- to 19-year-olds will also actually respond to messages at that time. One-third of smartphone users would rather go without sex than their smartphone. Fifty-three percent of 16-to 75-year-olds use their smartphone when walking and 11 percent of all respondents (21 percent of those aged 16 to 24) even admit to checking it when crossing the road. An Ofcom (UK telecommunications regulator) Communications Market Report published in July 2018 found that 71 percent of adults never turn off their phone and 78 percent feel they can't live without their phone.

All of these surveys paint a fairly dismal picture of smartphone user habits, which include risking sleep, intimate relationships, and potentially, life and limb in favor of checking the phone for whatever it might offer. Real-life experiences—including the threat of a car accident!—seem to pale compared to the lure of the virtual smartphone world.

---

6   Michael Winnick, "Putting a Finger on Our Phone Obsession," June 16, 2016, https://blog.dscout.com/mobile-touches.

7   Gabrielle Kratsas, "Cellphone Use Causes Over 1 in 4 Car Accidents," March 28, 2014, https://www.eu.usatoday.com/story/money/cars/2014/03/28/cellphone-use-1-in-4-car-crashes/7018505.

How Addicted Are You?

David Greenfield, PhD, an assistant clinical professor of psychiatry at the University of Connecticut School of Medicine and founder of the Center for Internet and Technology Addiction (CITA), developed the Smartphone Compulsion Test to provide insight into the extent of our smartphone dependency. Greenfield led the first large-scale study of internet use in 1999. His organization, CITA, conducts neurobiological and psychological research into internet and technology addiction, dependency, and abuse.

According to Greenfield, if you respond positively to 5 or more of the test's questions, then it's likely you have a problematic smartphone-use pattern. If you respond "yes" to 8 or more questions, then he recommends you seek professional help for behavioral addiction. He defines 1 to 2 yeses as "normal" smartphone use and 3 to 4 as "leaning toward problematic or compulsive use." It's interesting that checking yes to just 1 or 2 of the questions is defined as normal because I know of very few people who would be at that low level of usage. It seems that what's clinically defined as normal is actually pretty rare in Western society. Looking through these questions, I think most everyone I know feels somewhat anxious without their phone, wishes they could use it less, yet uses it while simultaneously walking/eating/or doing other activities. But what's become normal or acceptable to our minds is probably just because everyone else is doing it too.

Smartphone Compulsion Test

1. Do you find yourself spending more time on your cell or smartphone than you realize?	❏ YES	❏ NO
2. Do you find yourself mindlessly passing time on a regular basis by staring at your cell or smartphone?	❏ YES	❏ NO
3. Do you seem to lose track of time when on your cell or smartphone?	❏ YES	❏ NO
4. Do you find yourself spending more time texting, tweeting, or emailing as opposed to talking to people in person?	❏ YES	❏ NO
5. Has the amount of time you spend on your cell or smartphone been increasing?	❏ YES	❏ NO
6. Do you wish you could be a little less involved with your cell or smartphone?	❏ YES	❏ NO

7. Do you sleep with your cell or smartphone (turned on) under your pillow or next to your bed regularly?	❏ YES ❏ NO
8. Do you find yourself viewing and answering texts, tweets, and emails at all hours of the day and night—even when it means interrupting other things you are doing?	❏ YES ❏ NO
9. Do you text, email, tweet, or surf while driving or doing other similar activities that require your focused attention and concentration?	❏ YES ❏ NO
10. Do you feel your use of your cell or smartphone decreases your productivity at times?	❏ YES ❏ NO
11. Do you feel reluctant to be without your cell or smartphone, even for a short time?	❏ YES ❏ NO
12. Do you feel ill at ease or uncomfortable when you accidentally leave your smartphone in the car or at home, have no service, or have a broken phone?	❏ YES ❏ NO
13. When you eat meals, is your cell or smartphone always part of the table place setting?	❏ YES ❏ NO
14. When your cell or smartphone rings, beeps, or buzzes, do you feel an intense urge to check for texts, tweets, emails, updates, etc.?	❏ YES ❏ NO
15. Do you find yourself mindlessly checking your cell or smartphone many times a day, even when you know there is likely nothing new or important to see?	❏ YES ❏ NO

Yes responses:

1 to 2: "Normal" smartphone use

3 to 4: Leaning toward problematic behavior

5 or more: Likely problematic smartphone use

8 or more: Seeking professional help for behavioral addiction recommended

How did you do? My guess is that you're reading this book because you already identified you've got an issue with your technology use, so possibly, there were no surprises in your score. My advice is to retake the test in seven weeks (there's another copy in the Appendix on page 134), when you've finished reading the book and would like to see if your level of compulsion has dropped.

Why Do We Become Addicted?

Why do some people become addicted to things that others can try once but never do again or manage to consume in a moderate way? There have been many theories over the years. One is that addiction is passed on genetically, that it's an illness, and so the addict shouldn't be vilified but rather empathized with. The other school of thought is a more critical one, viewing addicts as lacking in sufficient self-control or willpower to stop whatever harmful activity they're engaged in.

The addicts I've worked with come from diverse backgrounds. Some were born into great wealth, others into poverty. Some are highly educated, others left school early without any qualifications. A family history of addiction was the case for some but not others.

Much research has been carried out over the past century on the nature of addiction, what causes it, and what can cure it. One study that I found particularly interesting was by Canadian professor of psychology Bruce Alexander on cocaine addiction.

Alexander's research coincided with an iconic antidrug ad featuring the same subjects (rats) and addictive substance (cocaine) that was broadcast in the US in 1980. The TV spot depicted a lab rat guzzling away on a bottle purportedly containing cocaine-laced water with a funereal voice-over stating, "Only one drug is so addictive that 9 out of 10 laboratory rats will use it and use it…until dead."

Alexander noticed that the rats being monitored for susceptibility to cocaine addiction in the ad were housed in solitary cages and had literally nothing to do but take the drugs. He wondered what might happen if they were given some alternatives. So he built Rat Park, a lush cage where the rats had colored balls, good food, tunnels to scamper down, and, crucially, plenty of cage mates. In Rat Park, all the rats tried both water bottles—one laced with cocaine, one without.

Unlike the rats in the ad, the rats of the gated Rat Park community preferred the pure water to the cocaine-laced version. The Rat Park cohort consumed in total less than a quarter of the drugs the isolated rats used, and none of them died. While all the rats that were alone became heavy users, none of the rats who had a richer, more varied environment did.

I should point out that there have been some academic challenges to certain aspects of Alexander's research. He purportedly lost eight days' worth of data due to a malfunction in a piece of equipment used to measure the amount of liquid the rats consumed, which may potentially have impacted his results. He also allegedly failed to take account of some important variables.[8] Those criticisms notwithstanding, when I read the findings of the experiment, they intuitively made a lot of sense to me in terms of the addicts I know. I've never met an addict who was happy and content with their life prior to succumbing to addiction, whether that was to alcohol, drugs, or gambling.

In his book, *Chasing the Scream: The First and Last Days of the War on Drugs*, Johann Hari outlines a human case study concerning Vietnam veterans that seems to back up the Rat Park experiment. During the Vietnam War, heroin use was quite commonplace among US soldiers, and an estimated 15 percent of them became addicts.[9] However, when they got home, only 5 percent of the formerly addicted men relapsed within a year, and just 12 percent relapsed within three years.[10] "Operation Golden Flow," as the recovery program was unofficially called, was uniquely successful in terms of heroin rehabilitation. The consensus seemed to be that the disruption to the environment jolted the addicts out of their substance abuse. When they arrived back home, they were in a completely different milieu, with a different crowd, in a totally different physical environment. Hari, however, argues that it was more to do with the fact that the soldiers had shifted "from a terrifying cage back to a pleasant one."

But What's This Got to Do with Smartphones?

All well and good, you say, but how is this connected with our use, or rather, our abuse of smartphones? When a person uses cocaine (or any other drug, including alcohol), it affects the central nervous system, stimulating neurotransmitter receptors in the brain's reward center, or nucleus accumbens. This triggers a huge release of dopamine, a feel-good chemical. The release of dopamine gives the user a rapid rush of energy and sensation of pleasure that radiates through their brain. This rewarding high leads them to desire more of their substance of choice so they can sustain or repeat the sensation.

In a similar way, it is hypothesized that smartphones can become addictive because they activate this same neurological reflex. Whenever a "user" receives a timely response to a

---

8   Katie MacBride, "This 38-Year-Old Study Is Still Spreading Bad Ideas about Addiction," *The Outline*, September 5, 2017, https://theoutline.com/post/2205/this-38-year-old-study-is-still-spreading-bad-ideas-about-addiction.

9   Sanjay Gupta, "Vietnam, Heroin, and the Lesson of Disrupting Any Addiction," *CNN*, December 23, 2015, https://edition-m.cnn .com/2015/12/21/health/vietnam-heroin-disrupting-addiction/index.html.

10   Gupta, "Vietnam, Heroin, and the Lesson of Disrupting Any Addiction."

text, an Instagram post like, or a hot Tinder match, they will likely feel a surge of pleasure and reward, suggesting that the neurons in the brain's reward center are releasing dopamine, making them feel good. If the behavior sparking this reward is repeated—posting pictures, swiping right on Tinder, sending instant messages—their dopamine levels may rise even higher and their brains send the message that this is a good activity, keep doing it!

Dopamine is necessary for survival, and it has served a valuable evolutionary purpose for the human race. Through it, our brains got rewarded for identifying an attractive mate with whom to procreate (ensuring we pass our genes on), finding food sources, forming social connections, and receiving recognition in our communities. As a species, we learned to repeat those activities again and again, thus reinforcing them and helping us to survive and prosper. The challenge with smartphones is that we're potentially overloaded, whether it's with images of attractive potential mates or tasty things to eat, and so we find it more difficult to discern what's necessary and nurturing for us and what's not.

This dopamine reward system evolved in the face of scarcity thousands of years ago when we might have had to travel long distances to find food, or indeed, a mate. But, now, our brains are bombarded with so many potential sources of dopamine that we need more intense hits from the pleasure sources located in our smartphones as our usage develops. This addictive tendency can be easily identified and even quantified by certain social media apps; for example, when you first signed up to Instagram or Facebook and started posting pictures, perhaps you were happy with 10 likes, but after a while, anything fewer than 50 seemed paltry. So you posted more, shared more, sacrificing more of your personal time and space to get the same hit, much the same way a coke addict does for their drug. Unlike cocaine, however, smartphone use is socially sanctioned; it's now common to see whole families "using" together, disconnected from each other yet uniformly "connected."

The weekend before I started writing this book, I read a news story that confirmed that the National Health Service (NHS) in the UK was to open its first internet addiction center in West London. The fact that the UK government is now recognizing this as an addiction and funding treatment is a huge sign of the times. Given that the smartphone is now the medium of choice for almost two-thirds of those accessing the internet in the US[11] and

---

11   Eric Enge, "Mobile vs. Desktop Usage in 2018: Mobile Takes the Lead," *Stone Temple,* April 27, 2018, https://www.stonetemple.com/mobile-vs-desktop-usage-study.

three-quarters in the UK,[12] it's clear that internet addiction and smartphone addiction are becoming increasingly synonymous.

Neuroplasticity and Your Habits

Drug addictions are often referred to as "drug habits." The use of the word "habit" is actually very apt as an addiction is basically a habitual behavior that's become so entrenched that everything else in the addict's life takes second place to their addiction. Hopefully, most of you have not sacrificed your family or your job to your smartphone use. Still, the idea of it as a habitual behavior, cemented by repeated rituals, is useful.

Neural pathways are basically connections between different brain structures. A lecturer of mine once used the analogy of ski runs when explaining neural pathways, which I found really helpful. A strong neural pathway is like a well-worn ski track. For example, I get up, I check my phone, and I use certain apps. The brain allows me to do this without much conscious thought because it's regular, it's routine. Trying to build a new behavior is a bit like going backcountry (off-piste) skiing. It requires more deliberate effort, more conscious navigation. However, the more you use that off-track route you've chosen, the easier it becomes to ski down, and at a certain point, it becomes your familiar main route. Thanks to the fact that the brain is a living, plastic organ, our neural pathways are flexible and we are capable of developing healthier habits over time.

Breaking Patterns

One of the key learnings from Operation Golden Flow was how a change in an addict's environment and routine could help break the addiction cycle.

Morning routine is crucial. It's the start of the day, and for many, this dictates how the rest of the day will be. When clients recount stories of their bad days, it often starts with something they've seen on their phone, what's perceived as a negative message from a loved one, a social media post concerning an ex, a rash email from their boss, or a bleak global news story. For these clients, anxiety levels have peaked before they've even left their beds. Of course, much of what happens to us or indeed around us—on a personal, local, national,

---

12 Ofcom, "The Communications Market Report 2018," accessed January 11, 2019, https://www.ofcom.org.uk/research-and-data/multi-sector-research/cmr/cmr-2018/interactive.

or global level—is outside of our sphere of influence. But there is a lot that is, including how we chose to start the day. So, what can you do? Here are some ideas.

- **Buy an alarm clock and keep your phone out of your room overnight.** Okay, you've probably read this one a hundred times. I know I have but it really does work. This strategy removes the excuse of "oh, but I need my phone as an alarm clock" and hopefully stretches out the time between waking up and phone checking.

- **Do something good for yourself before you switch on that phone.** Meditation is great to do first thing as it resets you for the day (more on that in Chapter 4). But mindfully drinking a good cup of coffee or having a nice long shower can also be a way of eking out some precious time for yourself before you start to let in the outside world.

- **Don't look at work emails before you get to the office, or, at the very least, until you get on the bus/train, etc.** Most of us aren't getting paid enough to do so. Interestingly, the people who are probably don't even need to be told this. For instance, neither Anna Wintour, Warren Buffett, nor Ed Sheeran owns a smartphone. And it doesn't seem to have harmed their careers! Some of you may feel an obligation to respond to emails out of office hours. I'll address putting more boundaries in place outside your office hours in the next chapter. But for now, even if you do nothing else, experiment with not checking work email before you leave the house, giving yourself some head space in the morning.

Wait Training

I've read many articles advocating going cold turkey on your smartphone (e.g., just switching off your phone for the weekend). For me, this is a little like the advice to start meditating for "just" five minutes. If you've ever sat down and tried to meditate for five minutes on your first attempt, you'll know in practice, for most of us, it's a really difficult thing to do. Our Western minds are used to stimulation, and if we set overly ambitious goals that we fail to meet, we can feel defeated and are very unlikely to climb back on the wagon. So instead, start by fencing off some time when you can feel you can reasonably go without your phone. It might still be difficult for you but choose a period of time that you feel is achievable. Start small and increase the "wait time" before you check your phone. For me, it started with leaving my phone at home when I took my dog for a walk. It was only 45 minutes but it was a start and my enjoyment of that uninterrupted period of time gave me a taste for more!

When I started weight training, my personal trainer would often diminish the weight of my dumbbells (something which my ego didn't like very much!) to make sure I had the technique 100 percent perfected before I proceeded to reach for the more impressive-looking weights! While it took a bit longer to get to my goal, I was confident that I wasn't going to injure myself. In a similar way, with wait training, you should start small, develop your confidence and technique, and over time, increase the wait 'til you next check your phone.

What Can We Learn from Cocaine-Addicted Lab Rats?

Getting back to the rats and their cocaine, think about your own smartphone use: What does it say about you? Are you a contented rat? This is the key point, for me, about addiction. To treat addiction properly and completely, a user must look at what's leading them to feel isolated and discontent, to feel that their life is a cage. Even if the addicted rat's cocaine source is removed, there's still the problem of the isolated cage. And so it is with us. Let's say we tackle the problem. Imagine we're really successful in managing our issue, even going so far as replacing our smartphone with a basic-feature phone so that we're liberated from the tantalizing, time-wasting apps that developers are pushing our way. Will we then feel content? Can it really be that easy?

Chapter 7 deals with contentment, how you start to unlock the cage you may be keeping yourself in. How you enrich your life so that the dopamine drip of smartphone content no longer seems as compelling.

I'll also address how a change of environment likely contributed to the unique success of Operation Golden Flow, how you break patterns and lay down new neural pathways that jolt you out of your routine. The goal of the second half of the book (Chapters 4 to 7) will not be reducing smartphone addiction per se but finding healthier sources of dopamine, increasing your focus and creativity, and maybe even increasing your fitness levels (as an added bonus!).

A NOTE ON PHONE ADDICTION

Time-consuming and limiting as an addiction to one's smartphone can be, it may be the tip of the iceberg. Smartphones are the most well-trodden access point to the World Wide Web, and, for some, that means a tantalizing gateway to porn, gambling, shopping, etc. If your issues include gambling, a shopping addiction, or compulsive porn-watching, then managing that goes beyond the framework of this book. The likelihood is if you get a handle on your phone use, you'll soon find another channel to get your fix. If this is your story then I would advise getting professional help and joining a local addict support group.

···················· EXERCISES ····················

Phone Usage Patterns (PUP)   Week 2

	Mon	Tue	Wed	Thu	Fri	Sat	Sun
Total estimated time							
Messaging, texting							
Calls							
Browsing							
Shopping							
Dating							
Facebook							
Instagram							
Twitter							
Porn							
Netflix, Amazon Prime, YouTube							
Gaming							
Other							

What were the feelings that came up today?

Monday:

_____

_____

Tuesday:

_____

_____

Wednesday:

_____

_____

Thursday:

_____

_____

Friday:

_____

_____

Saturday:

_____

_____

Sunday:

_____

_____

* * *

1. What did you try to reduce your phone use this week? Detail it here and rate its effectiveness on a scale of 0 to 10 (0 is totally useless, had no effect; 10 is totally effective).

_____

_____

_____

_____

_____

2. Wait training.

Choose one thing, one activity that you're going to do without your phone. During that time, it's either left at home or switched off. Guard that time and stick to it. Write it down here. Be specific—choose a time/activity that's totally off grid.

I'll be adding this into next week's PUP chart.

_____

_____

_____

3. Turn off alerts and notifications.

Alerts and notifications are for a smartphone addict what tempting sugary or salty snacks are for an overeater. Pinging, bleeping, buzzing come-hithers for dopamine cravers, they're like the treats you might feel tempted to consume even when you're not hungry, just because they're available and they're fresh. When people embark on a diet or healthy eating regimen, often the first thing they'll do is empty their cupboards of junk food so that it's not easily available. This exercise follows the same principle, removing some of the bait that threatens to distract you from your goal of spending less time on your phone!

List here the applications that you will turn off notifications for—ideally this would be all of them. But focus on the ones you can really stick with for now:

_____

_____

_____

_____

_____

4. Break patterns.

Choose at least one activity from Breaking Patterns (page 26) and commit to it for the rest of this course. Note how this affects you here, as well is in your weekly phone use journal. Once you embed this new activity into your daily routine, perhaps you will feel confident enough to add another one. For now, focus on committing to one new behavior.

_____

_____

_____

_____

_____

CHAPTER 3

The Corrosive Power of Being Always Available

"He switched off both his phones. A rare declaration, in a city like Lagos for a man like him, that she had his absolute attention."
—Chimamanda Ngozi Adichie in *Americanah*

Most of us like to be needed. It's a pretty basic human drive—to feel that our presence makes a difference to those around us. However, this drive can become destructive when our self-confidence depends on being needed by and indispensable to others to the extent that we will compromise ourselves to fulfill their every wish and whim.

When taken to an extreme, the need to be available to others (partners, friends, bosses, colleagues, children, parents, siblings) starts to look a lot like codependency. Codependency has become somewhat of a pop psychology buzzword in recent years, one applied to a wide spectrum of relational dysfunction. But at its core it means putting our own happiness into the hands of others and conversely assuming we are responsible for making those around us happy. What it looks like in practice is letting our boss's inability to switch off dictate our own working practices or not being able to say no to social invitations when we're totally exhausted for fear that another person might think ill of us. In short, it's constantly putting other peoples' needs ahead of our own, or worse, even denying we have needs of our own.

Smartphones are particularly enabling for fostering these codependent dynamics. I work with a lot of clients who have a constant drip feed of requests coming their way via their device, many endowed with a false sense of urgency. They feel unable to lay boundaries down with the result that they feel compelled to check their emails and messages last thing at night and first thing in the morning. One client, whose boss is based several continents away, even added in a middle-of-the-night check "to keep on top of things." At the root of this wasn't so much concern for the work per se but my client's need to be liked, valued, appreciated, and, crucially, depended upon.

Always Working but Not Always Productive

The compulsion to be "always on," always available does not equate to increased productivity. According to the latest Organization for Economic Cooperation and Development (OECD) index, Luxembourg, the most productive country, has an average work week of just 29 hours. The US is ranked just sixth, with the four European countries ahead of it—Luxembourg, Denmark, Norway, and Switzerland—putting in significantly fewer working hours.[13]

Jennifer Pinches, a former Olympic athlete, wrote for Expert Market, "It may be counterintuitive to view downtime as beneficial to generating value efficiently, but many business skills ranging from communication to decision-making are worsened by the fatigue of working long hours."[14]

In the '80s, Gordon Gekko, the antihero of the movie *Wall Street*, proclaimed that lunch was for wimps. It's clear that a culture of glorifying employees for working long hours to the detriment of their personal life or health existed long before the advent of the smartphone. Before the internet and the smartphone, however, there were limits as to how much work you could do when physically removed from the office. Now, the most modest smartphone can do infinitely more than the 1980s mainframe computer. So, we carry our tools sharpened and ready with us everywhere. Neither time nor geography can limit us, and that's a big challenge for those of us trying to hold on to some semblance of personal time.

---

13 Jennifer Pinches, "The World's Most Productive Countries," Expert Market, accessed January 11, 2019, https://www.expertmarket.co.uk/focus/worlds-most-productive-countries-2017.

14 Pinches, "The World's Most Productive Countries."

Productivity in the US and UK stopped growing at the time of the financial crisis in 2008–09, after having climbed steadily from 1922 onward. What else happened in 2008? I'm no economist, but it's hard to ignore the impact of the iPhone, which had launched in the second half of 2007 and by 2008 was becoming more mainstream, changing our work and personal lives forever.

"Cell phone and texting" was identified as the biggest productivity killer at work by employers in a 2016 CareerBuilder study.[15] The next biggest distraction was "the internet." Interestingly, the study also found that 82 percent of employees keep their smartphone within eye contact at work. Another piece of research, this time carried out by the Universities of Würzburg and Nottingham Trent,[16] supports this link between productivity and smartphone presence. Researchers asked participants to perform a concentration test in four different scenarios: with their smartphone in their pocket, on their desk, locked away in a drawer, and in another room. The results are significant. Test results were lowest when the smartphone was on the desk, but with every additional layer of distance between participants and their smartphones, test performance increased. Overall, test results were 26 percent higher when phones were removed from the room. It's clear that even the mere physical proximity of a switched-off smartphone can interfere with our ability to get on with a task in hand.

Debunking Work Myths

I've worked with many clients to help them try to achieve more work-life balance. For one client, the goal was to draw some boundaries around her weekend and to stop taking work home to complete on Saturdays and Sundays. It was challenging for her to break this habit, which she had built up through a decade of her working life. However, when she finally got there, she was astonished to find that her productivity did not suffer; in fact, her Monday to Friday work week became more fruitful. This client is a creative, and by taking a step away from her normal work for two days she was able to spend some time nurturing herself—meditating, visiting galleries, and taking walks in nature, and this investment in herself allowed her creativity to flow more freely through her work.

---

15   CareerBuilder, "New CareerBuilder Survey Reveals How Much Smartphones Are Sapping Productivity at Work," June 9, 2016, http://www.careerbuilder.com/share/aboutus/pressreleasesdetail.aspx?sd=6%2F9%2F2016&id=pr954&ed=12%2F31%2F2016.

16   Kaspersky Lab. "Kaspersky Lab Study Proves Smartphones Distract Workers and Decrease Productivity," August 26, 2016, https://usa.kaspersky.com/about/press-releases/2016_kaspersky-lab-study-proves-smartphones-distract-workers-and-decrease-productivity.

Conversely, when she worked all weekend, she'd drag herself to work drained and resentful on Monday mornings.

Another client harbored an anxiety that if she stopped checking her phone for work email around the clock (this was the one who did the middle-of-the-night checks from her bed), her boss would think she was lazy and it would be the first step toward getting fired. We explored the validity of this belief, and together, we slowly began to dismantle her fear. The final straw came, however, when her sleep pattern became so erratic (no doubt due to her being on her phone at 3 a.m.) that she could barely get through the day and was taking her exhaustion and frustration out on her partner. She realized that the cost of her always-on work ethic was too high, and she was heading for a crash.

So, we worked on how she would communicate to her boss that she was going to be adopting a new working style, where she would no longer be checking email between certain hours and not at all over the weekend (unless this was previously discussed and negotiated ahead of a big launch, for instance). Initially, her boss was taken aback as it was quite a turnaround for my client to speak out about her own needs or priorities (to spend more time with her family and friends), but she ultimately supported her. Nevertheless, as time went on, her challenge was not her boss insisting she pick up work out of hours but rather that she stick to her own intention! After a couple of stumbles, however, she managed to find her stride very well and her restricted work style became the new normal. She related how surprised she was that she was actually getting through more rather than less work. Previously, she'd surf the internet or chat with friends on WhatsApp to distract herself from tasks she didn't want to do, knowing that, ultimately, she could make up the time later by working on her phone or tablet, either on the train or on the couch while half watching TV with her partner. However, when she knew her day would end at 5.30 p.m., she focused more on the task at hand, which not only freed up time for herself later but gave her a sense of accomplishment and completion.

The second benefit was she got into the habit of asking for things and articulating her needs, something that she previously thought was pointless or, worse, potential evidence that she wasn't committed to the job! By asking for what she wanted without it having a negative outcome, my client became more confident. For the first time she went into her review meeting with a list of requests rather than passively lying in wait for feedback from her boss. There was a shift in dynamic with her boss, who started to respect and value her as an equal rather than someone to just pile work onto. My client also found the ability to say no to certain requests when it would jeopardize her ability to competently carry out tasks that were already on her plate.

You might argue that your boss expects you to do X or Y and that you have no choice, that the way they work dictates how you work, even if it means leaving your phone on while on vacation. Others feel it's up to their boss to notice how exhausted they look, how they keep getting ill due to overworking. This, again, is a codependent mentality of "I give you my all, I overlook my own needs, but in return you intuit those needs and make moves to fulfill them." This thinking ultimately leads to a reservoir of resentment; we feel shortchanged when we don't get the recognition, the accolades, or the promotions we feel we deserve in exchange for the sacrifices we have made. But it is ultimately up to you and no one else to listen to your body and to put healthy boundaries in place to protect your health and well-being.

Placing Our Relationships On Hold

When it comes to our personal relationships, many of us feel like we should be reachable by anyone at any time, that we must respond in near real time or face the consequences—not being valued or liked. The irony is that statistics point to increased levels of loneliness, disconnection, and anxiety among heavy social media and smartphone users. As one of my clients put it, "Check my Insta, I have thousands of followers but no one knows what's really going on with me." This client's marriage was on the brink of collapse, and she was feeling intense grief following the death of a close family member several years before. But no one knew.

According to recent figures from the Office for National Statistics,[17] in the UK almost 10 percent of 16- to 24-year-olds admit to feeling lonely "often or always"—almost double the proportion of those over 64 who said the same. The younger group contains the heaviest users of social media and smartphones yet is the cohort that feels most isolated. According to the findings, those who felt the loneliest were more likely to use technology compulsively.[18]

---

17   Edward Pyle and Dani Evans, "Loneliness—What Characteristics and Circumstances Are Associated with Feeling Lonely?" *Office for National Statistics,* accessed February 17, 2019, https://www.ons.gov.uk/peoplepopulationandcommunity/wellbeing/articles/lonelinesswhatcharacteristicsandcircumstancesareassociatedwithfeelinglonely/2018-04-10.

18   Natalie Gil, "2,000 Young British People Were Asked About Loneliness—Here's What They Found," *Refinery 29,* April 23, 2018, https://www.refinery29.uk/2018/04/197145/loneliness-young-people.

This trend is also seen among US millennials. A study conducted by San Francisco State University on student phone usage and mental health found that those with the highest level of phone use reported feeling more lonely and isolated than peers less dependent on their devices. The most frequent users also displayed higher levels of depression and anxiety.

What's clear is that most of us are now very aware of the impact our smartphone use is having on our relationships. Some interesting statistics to consider:

- Half of those aged 18 to 34 think going cold turkey would have a positive effect on their real-world relationships and mental health.[19]

- One in three people argue with their partner over phone use.[20]

- In a 2017 survey of 143 women in committed relationships, 75 percent said that smartphones had a destructive effect on their relationship.

It's clear we're paying a high price for our availability. We are everywhere but rarely are we fully present anywhere. Phone use, digital distraction, lack of attentiveness—these are perennial topics in my couples work. I sometimes wonder if the phone hasn't replaced the "other woman/man" as top relationship threat.

Clients most commonly express having time and space to think and reflect as one of the main benefits of coming to therapy. I believe a key factor in creating this space is the fact that phones are off. For 50 minutes two people (or three for couples work) are present and available to one another without interruption. It's a sacred space and a pretty rare occurrence in this day and age, when we're used to bleeping, buzzing, and vibrating noises trespassing on our interactions with others. One of my clients recently told me that his 50-minute therapy session was the only time during the week that he switched his phone off. Even when he slept, he kept it on low vibrate. Renowned psychotherapist Irvin Yalom wrote of the therapeutic process in his book *Existential Psychotherapy*: "It is the relationship that heals." I strongly believe that the attentiveness and focus shown to the client without external distractions is the key to building this strong working bond between therapist and client.

19   Royal Society for Public Health, "Status of Mind: Social Media and Young People's Mental Health and Well-Being," accessed January 11, 2019, https://www.rsph.org.uk/uploads/assets/uploaded/62be270a-a55f-4719-ad668c2ec7a74c2a.pdf.

20   Deloitte, "2017 Global Mobile Consumer Survey," https://www2.deloitte.com/us/en/pages/technology-media-and-telecommunications/articles/global-mobile-consumer-survey-us-edition.html.

When It Starts to Hit Home

One of my clients started to grasp the impact his smartphone habit was having on his family life when his eight-year-old daughter presented him with a beautifully illustrated portrait of the entire family. In it, he was depicted slightly apart from the rest of the clan, with his smartphone clenched in his hand. He already knew on some level that he had an issue, particularly with work email out of hours, but seeing it through his daughter's eyes was the wake-up call he needed to start to make some changes and to draw boundaries around the precious time he spent with his family.

Another couple I worked with no longer kissed or hugged each other first thing in the morning and both acutely missed this start to the day. I asked when those signs of affection started to wane. Both said "smartphones." The wife said that they no longer looked at each other much because 95 percent of the time they were looking at their screens. Her husband nodded assent. She added that her two-year-old daughter had become so frustrated by her constantly phone use, she started telling her, "Mommy, no phone." It's clear that by opting to be "always on" for whatever flashes up on our smartphones, we're switching off in our most important relationships and are unavailable to those we value most.

What's your wake-up call?

EXERCISES

Phone Usage Patterns (PUP)   **Week 3**

	Mon	Tue	Wed	Thu	Fri	Sat	Sun
Total estimated time							
Messaging, texting							
Calls							
Browsing							
Shopping							
Dating							
Facebook							
Instagram							
Twitter							
Porn							
Netflix, Amazon Prime, YouTube							
Gaming							
Other							

	Mon	Tue	Wed	Thu	Fri	Sat	Sun
Wait training: Note your phone-free activities or periods that you went without your phone.							

What were the feelings that came up today?

Monday: _____

_____

Tuesday: _____

_____

Wednesday: _____

_____

Thursday: _____

_____

Friday: _____

_____

Saturday: _____

_____

Sunday: _____

_____

* * *

1. What did you try to reduce your phone use this week? Detail it here and rate its effectiveness on a scale of 0 to 10 (0 is totally useless, had no effect; 10 is totally effective).

_____

_____

_____

_____

2. Cut data allowance.

The most basic and surefire way to curtail smartphone use is slashing your data package. I learned this after a long weekend spent without WiFi in the South of France last summer. Upon returning home mid-month, my monthly data allowance had been used up thanks to WiFi deprivation. So, I faced two weeks without data apart from when I was at home or at work. It was great! I didn't need to stop myself from sneaking a look on Instagram or googling a random something while I was on the go. Cutting back on data is a double win. You save money and save time you might have wasted away on your phone!

Each mobile operator has a different policy around this but by and large they would rather you cut down your allowance than leave, so you can always play hardball to get what you want. You may fear that reducing your data package will just have you hopping from one WiFi zone to the next. I can honestly say this wasn't my experience as I easily tired of the endless form-filling required and the bartering away of personal details in exchange for connectivity. Limiting your data access pretty much guarantees an end to "always on." Try it!

Questions to ask your operator:

- What are the options to reduce your data allowance?

- If it's not possible to change it right away, when is the next available date you can make this change (note that as a calendar reminder)? If they're being very inflexible and trying to offer you more rather than less, explain that you will be looking at other operators to see what they can offer; this in my experience, usually encourages them to be way more flexible!

Write what you intend to do with that money saved. Make it meaningful and specific to you. It could be that you start to build some savings, donate to your favorite charity, or buy something beautiful for yourself. If you start to see a benefit to yourself in this way, your intention will feel less deprivational, and thus, easier to stick to.

_____

_____

_____

_____

3. Verbalize your intent.

Whether it's having a chat with your boss about what your boundaries are going to be around phone use after hours or with your partner about keeping the phone out of the bedroom, it really helps to speak those words aloud so those who will be impacted by your new relationship with your phone can witness them.

With regard to work, this is particularly important if your boss is used to having you pick up emails at all hours and even on vacation. Let them know you will no longer be "always on," but instead plan to be more present during the actual hours that you are contracted to work.

Many people feel intimidated about having such a frank conversation with their supervisor, particularly if there's been a strong "always on" work precedent. In such cases it may be helpful to consider the following:

- Explain that you want to try a different style of working. Set a trial period, say one month, and suggest you and your boss meet at the end of the month to see what effect the boundaried style had on your work. Being proactive and offering to be accountable shows that you're taking your goal seriously but want to stay on top of the impact on your deliverables. Note the key points to your new working style:

_____

_____

_____

_____

- Outline the rationale for your proposal. This should include the impact the "always on" style has on how you approach work, your energy levels, and your enthusiasm. Contrast this with how you want to be at work (e.g., focused, engaged, and rested).

_____

_____

_____

_____

- Be clear on what you propose. What are you offering? What do you expect in return?

_____

_____

_____

_____

- Clarify any exceptions to the rule. For instance, my client who made the decision to only work within office hours did outline some caveats to her boss. Twice per year they'd have a big corporate announcement and she agreed to work more flexibly during the week prior to both those announcements. Be specific on the exceptions you sign up for, and make sure they're just that—exceptions rather than the rule.

_____

_____

_____

_____

4. Manage expectations via the social media and chat apps you use.

I noticed recently that my default setting is "available" on my WhatsApp. So, for close to the past decade I've theoretically been always available to my WhatsApp contacts. Talk about misleading and unrealistic! I recently changed that to "Not always on. If urgent, call!" It serves as a reminder to myself as well as to others that I am not always available. About 90 percent of my WhatsApp address book is "available" all the time. Reflect on what your status is and what you'd like it to be:

_____

_____

_____

_____

Update your chat app(s) accordingly.

5. Unsubscribe from all group chats you don't want to be on.

Group chats are notorious time and battery guzzlers that typically hook us into things we don't want to do and conversations we're not interested in. Sort the wheat out from the chaff. Remember, your time is limited and precious.

Reflect on what chats are meaningful/useful to you and which are time-wasting or energy-draining. Write down here which you intend to delete and why. I'll be checking in with you at the end of the book to see whether you made the right choice. If it's easier (and you don't feel like making a point of exiting the group), then think about muting the conversations for now.

_____

_____

_____

_____

6. Focus on being available to the people whose company you're actually in.

The best way of doing this is simply switching your phone off when you're socializing or spending quality time with your partner or children. I used to place my phone on silent mode when out with friends but I'd regularly take a sneaky peak at it when they went to the bathroom or to the bar. Invariably, I'd respond to a message, get briefly involved in a chat, and then mentally be in a completely different place when my friend returned. When I have my phone switched off, I find I'm less tempted to do this; it's simply not worth the hassle.

Consider situations where you sometimes reach for your phone when you wish you didn't. For you it might be when you're at the playground with your kid or when you're at the movies. Commit to switching off your phone completely on one of these occasions for the duration of reading this book.

Three situations where I am distracted by phone but wish I could be more present:

1. _____

2. _____

3. _____

Now choose one of the three situations and insert it in the sentence below.

I am going to commit to not using my phone when I _____
until I complete this book/6 weeks (for speed readers!).

CHAPTER 4

Smarter Phones, Dumber Users: How Your Phone Might Be Changing the Way You Think

"Once a new technology rolls over you, if you're not part of the steamroller, you're part of the road."

—Stewart Brand, writer and editor of the *Whole Earth Catalog*

I worked in technology PR at the turn of the millennium. At that time the advent of the $100 laptop by the One Laptop per Child (OLPC) Foundation envisaged a bright new future where each schoolchild in the developing world would be armed with a shiny new laptop, a gateway to previously unimaginable learning opportunities that would democratize education globally.

Fast-forward almost two decades and the gloss has gone off the OLPC initiative. A 2013 study in Uruguay, where every primary schoolchild received a free laptop in 2009,[21] concluded that the laptops did not improve literacy and were mainly used for recreation, with

---

21   "The Impact of a One Laptop per Child Program on Learning: Evidence from Uruguay," 2017, https://digital.fundacionceibal.edu.uy/jspui/bitstream/123456789/181/1/The%20impact%20of%20a%20One%20Laptop%20per%20Child%20Program_final%20%283%29.pdf.

only 4.1 percent of the laptops being used "all" or "most" days during the 2012 academic year. The main conclusion was that the OLPC program had no impact on the test scores in reading and math. Tellingly, the technology elite themselves remain unconvinced about the power of connected devices to educate, at least for their own progeny. Silicon Valley's prestigious Waldorf School, which is responsible for educating the offspring of eBay's CTO and that of many senior employees of Google, Apple, Yahoo, and Hewlett-Packard, eschews tech tools in favor of pens and paper, knitting needles, and occasionally, mud. According to a *New York Times* article on the school, "Not a computer to be found. No screens at all. They are not allowed in the classroom, and the school even frowns on their use at home."[22]

Paul Thomas, a former teacher and an associate professor of education at Furman University, who has written many books on public educational methods, supports the Waldorf philosophy, saying "a sparse approach to technology in the classroom will always benefit learning...Teaching is a human experience. Technology is a distraction when we need literacy, numeracy, and critical thinking."[23]

Andrew Mellor, president of the UK's National Association of Head Teachers (NAHT), recently expressed the opinion that children were entering schools as passive rather than active learners due to the technology devices they use. He said that iPads and tablets, which are increasingly being used by children under five, were preventing children from developing their imagination and curiosity. He commented, "They have not been stimulated in early reading and maths but essentially had an iPad in front of them rather than looking through books and developing vocabulary."[24]

Two of the biggest names in technology—Bill Gates and Steve Jobs—both limited their children's exposure to the very tech they invented. Gates, the former CEO of Microsoft, implemented a cap on screen time when his daughter started developing an unhealthy attachment to a video game. He also didn't let his children get cell phones until they turned 14 (the average age for an American child getting their first phone is 10).[25] Jobs, CEO (until a couple of months before his death in 2011) and cofounder of Apple, banned

---

22   Matt Richtel, "A Silicon Valley School That Doesn't Compute," *The New York Times*, October 22, 2011, https://www.nytimes.com/2011/10/23/technology/at-waldorf-school-in-silicon-valley-technology-can-wait.html.

23   Richtel, "A Silicon Valley School That Doesn't Compute."

24   Bhvishya Patel, "iPads Don't Necessarily Put the I Back in Intelligence Says Country's Biggest Teaching Union, with Schoolchildren Staying Glued to Screens Rather Than Using Their Imagination," *The Daily Mail*, September 8, 2018, http://www.dailymail.co.uk/news/article-6146005/iPads-dont-necessarily-intelligence-says-countrys-biggest-teaching-union.html.

25   Influence Central, "Kids & Tech: The Evolution of Today's Digital Natives," accessed January 11, 2019, http://influence-central.com/kids-tech-the-evolution-of-todays-digital-natives.

his own children from using the then newly released iPad and explained in 2010: "We limit how much technology our kids use at home."[26] Jobs's biographer gave another interesting insight into their family life: "Every evening Steve made a point of having dinner at the big long table in their kitchen, discussing books and history and a variety of things. No one ever pulled out an iPad or computer. The kids did not seem addicted at all to devices."[27]

What did Jobs and Gates—two of the brightest minds of our age—know about the dangers of technology that they wanted to protect their kids from? Instinctively, the link between increasingly smart devices and increasingly "dumb" users makes sense to me. After all, on a basic level our brains are muscles. If we neglect to train and work out those muscles by being overdependent on our smartphones (relying on them to remember important dates, facts, or directions, etc.), they get flabby, just as our bodies do when we are inactive.

Unfortunately, at this point, longitudinal research on the impact of heavy smartphone use on brain chemistry isn't available. The devices simply haven't been around long enough. I believe several key brain functions, however, are impeded by heavy smartphone use: our ability to pay attention, to be creative, to focus, and possibly most important of all, to switch off and do nothing!

Four Smart Reasons to Switch Off Your Phone

Reason 1: To Pay Attention

Why is attention so important? As the first step in the learning process, it is pretty much essential for our growth and development. We cannot understand, learn, or remember that which we do not first attend to.[28]

Attention has two key functions: executive and alarming. The first is active and guided by alertness, concentration, and interest. Executive is the form of attention I need for writing this book! The alarming function is more passive. It's an involuntary process directed by

---

26   Nick Bilton, "Steve Jobs Was a Low-Tech Parent," *The New York Times,* September 10, 2014, https://www.nytimes.com/2014/09/11/fashion/steve-jobs-apple-was-a-low-tech-parent.html.

27   Sarah Berger, "Tech-free Dinners and No Smartphones Past 10 PM—How Steve Jobs, Bill Gates, and Mark Cuban Limited Their Kids' Screen Time," *CNBC,* June 5, 2018, https://www.cnbc.com/2018/06/05/how-bill-gates-mark-cuban-and-others-limit-their-kids-tech-use.html.

28   Glenda Thorne and Alice Thomas, "What Is Attention?" *The Center for Development & Learning,* June 1, 2009, https://www.cdl.org/articles/what-is-attention.

external events that stand out from their environment, such as a bright flash, a strong odor, or a sudden loud noise. In other words, it appeals to our senses. As mentioned in the last chapter, we've now become so primed for alerts emanating from our smartphones that even when our phones are switched off but close, they diminish our executive attention faculty. Going back to my process of writing this book, it's the alarming function that can threaten to derail me when I'm writing. However, it's not that one is better than another. The alarming function is extremely valuable in certain situations and serves an important evolutionary function. If our ancestors' antennae weren't up and aroused by sudden noises such as the charge of dangerous beasts, then we simply wouldn't exist! Unfortunately, the part of our brain that responds to sudden noises or vibrations is still hardwired to prioritize that over whatever other task we're attending to for fear our lives might be at stake.

Reason 2: To Be Creative

Most of my ideas for this book came to me while I was well away from my laptop, and often when my reference books were gathering sand at the bottom of my suitcase. In other words, when my executive attention was switched off. Wandering aimlessly through the park with my dog, gazing out of a train window, eavesdropping on other peoples' conversations while on a layover at LAX were when many of my ideas came to me. I'm not alone. Albert Einstein attributed most of his best inventions to daydreaming and intuition: "All great achievements of science must start from intuitive knowledge. I believe in intuition and inspiration. I am enough of an artist to draw freely upon my imagination. Imagination is more important than knowledge. Knowledge is limited. Imagination encircles the world."[29]

A couple of years back I went to a talk by Rod Judkins, a professor at Central Saint Martins, one of the world's most famous art schools, attended by many illustrious creatives, including Alexander McQueen, Lucian Freud, and Stella McCartney, to name a few. In his talk, Judkins shared some concepts from his book *Ideas Are Your Only Currency*. Judkins argued that in this age of advanced technology where there is much anxiety over the development of AI (artificial intelligence) and many jobs becoming obsolete, our creativity will be the only thing that can differentiate us from increasingly smart technology. Judkins urged us to engage our creativity, to train it: "An Olympic athlete trains their body. A creative person has to exercise as hard, but train their imagination."

---

29 Alice Calaprice, *The Expanded Quotable Einstein* (Princeton, New Jersey: Princeton University Press, 2000).

I often explore creativity with my clients, curious to know what their creative channels are. Many say, "Oh, I'm just not creative." These beliefs are often rooted in feedback they've received as children from parents or teachers. But we all have the capacity to be creative. As Picasso said, "Every child is an artist. The problem is how to remain an artist once he grows up." If you've ever traveled in the developing world, you'll see how the kids can adapt so many abandoned objects into playthings; a tire becomes a float, tin cans are reinvented as something to paint on and decorate or repurpose as a pair of stilts. In the absence of ready-made things to amuse them, they create. It's incredibly inspiring as well as humbling to observe. Unfortunately, in the West, we're going in the other direction. As our phones become more engaging, we risk consuming more and more data, content, and games, and we create less. We get out of the habit of entertaining ourselves or each other. As one of the participants in a 2013 study on the impact of smartphones on college students said: "If I'm bored I can just download whatever I want and just sit there and play. I really cannot get bored using it. Before I would always get bored and I would have to find something else to do and that would involve, like, going somewhere or playing sports or doing something."[30]

I worked with a client who, becoming aware of the vast amounts of time that she dwindled away on social media apps (her smartphone drug of choice), decided to go cold turkey and delete all of them, using her phone exclusively for making calls. As a result, she found herself with several free hours in her day. She started to experiment with sewing and calligraphy, two things she enjoyed as a child but had given up many decades before. After reengaging with this long-neglected creative outlet, she found she had more energy both outside and within work. She related how hours would go by and she would get completely lost in what she was doing. She found great joy in doing something totally different from her day job. She eventually reinstalled her social media apps, this time editing whom she followed to reflect her new interests (i.e., harnessing the power of social media to inspire and spark her creativity rather than as a time-killing tool).

For each person, the creative channel will be different. After being told for a solid decade that I was no good at art, I abandoned my paintbrushes at around the age of 14. However, a couple of years ago I signed up for a painting course. I figured I had nothing to lose. I had zero expectations of myself; I just went to see what would happen, how it would be. My talent hadn't mystically improved during the intervening couple of decades, but I noticed

---

30 A. Lepp, J. Barkley, et al., "The Relationship between Cell Phone Use, Physical and Sedentary Activity, and Cardiorespiratory Fitness in a Sample of US College Students," *International Journal of Behavioral Nutrition and Physical Activity* 10, No. 79 (2013), doi: 10.1186/1479-5868-10-79.

how my attitude toward my output did. I remember getting frustrated as a teenager about how I couldn't accurately represent what I was seeing. This time I was kinder to myself. I reminded myself I was there because I chose to be there, I wasn't being graded, and that I could just experiment.

Reason 3: To Focus

Thanks to our omnipresent smartphones, the opportunities for us to multitask are greater than they ever have been. It's rare to see anyone focusing on just one thing, aka "mono tasking" any more. But what toll is this taking on our brains and our well-being? Up until very recently multitasking was seen as a strength. It was also seen as something women could do but men could not. However, research carried out over the past couple of decades has debunked many multitasking myths.

Firstly, most of us cannot multitask effectively. Stanford University research puts that figure at 97.5 percent of the population.[31] The other 2.5 percent have freakish abilities; scientists call them "super taskers" because they can actually successfully do more than one thing at once. They can drive while talking on the phone, without compromising their ability to react to others around them or shift gears. That's the point—not compromising their ability. When I first did some reading on the downside of multitasking, I started to observe how I constantly switched between tasks. Prior to this, I considered myself a deft, efficient multitasker and, being a woman, I fed on the belief that it was my birthright! But over time, I began to notice that when I paused my writing to respond to an email (and maybe to tweet while I was at it), I'd come back to what was my main task, my writing, with a sense of fogginess and a definite dip in the momentum I'd had previously.

Anthony Wagner, one of the Stanford professors involved in the research, describes what happens to the less successful multitaskers when they're distracted (and remember, that is almost 98 percent of us!): "When they're in situations where there are multiple sources of information coming from the external world or emerging out of memory, they're not able to filter out what's not relevant to their current goal. That failure to filter means they're slowed down by that irrelevant information." After putting about 100 students through a series of three tests, the researchers realized those heavy media multitaskers were paying

---

31 Adam Gorlick, "Media Multitaskers Pay Mental Price, Stanford Study Shows," *Stanford News,* August 24, 2009, https://news.stanford .edu/2009/08/24/multitask-research-study-082409.

a big mental price. "They're suckers for irrelevancy," said Professor Clifford Nass, another of the researchers. "Everything distracts them."

Earl Miller, a neuroscientist at MIT who focuses on divided attention, says that our brains are not wired to multitask well: "When people think they're multitasking, they're actually just switching from one task to another very rapidly. And every time they do, there's a cognitive cost in doing so."[32]

As Guy Winch, PhD, author of *Emotional First Aid: Practical Strategies for Treating Failure, Rejection, Guilt, and Other Everyday Psychological Injuries*, explains: "Moving back and forth between several tasks actually wastes productivity, because your attention is expended on the act of switching gears—plus, you never get fully 'in the zone' for either activity."[33]

In his book *The Organized Mind*, Daniel Levitin describes multitasking as the "ultimate empty-caloried brain candy." Instead of reaping the rewards that come from a sustained, focused effort, he says, we instead reap empty rewards from completing a thousand little sugarcoated tasks.[34] This really resonated with me. It was easy to set aside the writing of a book that wouldn't see the light of day for the better part of another year in favor of a timely tweet that would hopefully get a few likes!

> *"When people think they're multitasking, they're actually just switching from one task to another very rapidly. And every time they do, there's a cognitive cost in doing so."*
>
> —Earl Miller, MIT neuroscientist

Attempting to multitask throws many of us into fight-or-flight mode. Faced with an avalanche of work emails, news alerts, and personal chat streams, we're constantly deciding which to leave and which to tackle, all of which takes a toll, increasing the level of the stress hormone cortisol in our bodies. When University of California Irvine researchers measured the heart rates of employees with and without constant access to office email, they found that those who received a steady stream of messages stayed in a perpetual "high alert"

---

32   Daniel Levitin, *The Organized Mind* (London: Penguin, 2015), 96.

33   *The Huffington Post*. "Women Are Better Than Men at Multitasking, Study Says," January 01, 2017, https://www.huffingtonpost.ca/2017/01/27/multitasking-women-men_n_14435986.html#gallery/563137/1.

34   Levitin, *The Organized Mind*, 97.

mode with higher heart rates. Those without constant email access did less multitasking and were less stressed.[35]

The first step in training your brain to attend to whatever task you have at hand is to shut down all the external distractions that you can control. Number one is your smartphone. If you wish to write, to focus, to plan, to sort—in short, if you wish to do anything or indeed when you plan to do absolutely nothing—switch off *your* phone.

When I'm writing this book, my phone is in a different room, switched off, and my email is shut down. I recommend you do the same. I was well into Chapter 2 before I imposed these rules on myself. Before that I was all over the place. What started off as legitimate research would via hyperlink hopscotch evolve into another topic, totally unrelated to what I was supposed to be focusing on. The Pomodoro Technique is a useful tool that I discovered, which helped me to train my mind to focus for short bursts. A time-management method developed by Francesco Cirillo in the late 1980s, it uses a timer to break down work into intervals, traditionally 25 minutes in length, separated by short breaks. You can buy a physical Pomodoro timer (Pomodoro is Italian for tomato, and the timers are in the shape of a juicy red tomato!) or use the online version (tomato-timer.com).

The idea is that you work for 25 minutes then take a break for 5 or 10 minutes. It certainly helped to train me into focusing concertedly for 25 minutes. Trying to train myself to focus for a certain period of time was a bit like riding a bike, the timer providing the stabilizers to support and keep me on the right track. I used it for a couple of weeks but after that I found I had internalized the technique. It's still useful, though, for tasks from which I am more likely to get distracted.

A technique that works particularly well with the Pomodoro Technique is OHIO. Nothing to do with the American state, it stands for Only Handle It Once. Often prescribed for those with ADHD, in this age of mass distraction it's something most of us could benefit from. It essentially means if you take something on, you don't leave it until you complete it or at least a section of it that you designate at the outset. For me, it might be a subsection of this book or to design one set of exercises completely from beginning to end. Multitasking and OHIO are mutually exclusive!

35   Janet Wilson, "Email 'Vacations' Decrease Stress, Increase Concentration," *UCI News*, May 7, 2012, https://news.uci.edu/2012/05/07/email-vacations-decrease-stress-increase-concentration.

Reading a physical book, whether for enjoyment or learning (or both) is a good exercise in mono tasking! Reading on paper has two key advantages over a screen. Firstly, having a sense of where the text is positioned on the page has been shown to lead to better recall and comprehension. When scrolling down a screen, we don't get any sense of this. Secondly, the opportunities for media multitasking are higher if we're accessing reading material through a device from which we can also access social media, dating, shopping, and browsing possibilities. If we are reading a physical book and wish to do those things then it takes a much more conscious effort to put that book down, root out our phone, switch it on, etc. Probably for this very reason, reading time for e-books has been shown to be significantly longer than for physical books.

TIMED FOCUS

Here are two methods to train yourself to focus for a specific period of time:

1. **Pomodoro Technique.** Work for 25 minutes, then take a break for 5 or 10 minutes. You can buy a physical Pomodoro timer or use an online timer to schedule your breaks.

2. **Only Handle It Once (OHIO)** method. If you take something on, don't leave it until you complete it or at least a section of it that you designate at the outset.

It's interesting to note that after reaching a peak in 2014 there has recently been a dip in e-book sales, with hardbacks enjoying a resurgence. The latest figures from the The Publishers Association (US) showed e-book sales falling 17 percent in 2016, with an 8 percent rise in their physical counterparts. CEO of The Publishers Association (US), Stephen Lotinga attributed this to people getting tired of looking at screens. "There is generally a sense that people are now getting screen tiredness, or fatigue, from so many devices being used, watched, or looked at in their week. [Printed] books provide an opportunity to step away from that."[36]

---

36 Mark Sweney, "'Screen Fatigue' Sees UK E-book Sales Plunge 17% as Readers Return to Print," *The Guardian,* April 27, 2017, https://www.theguardian.com/books/2017/apr/27/screen-fatigue-sees-uk-ebook-sales-plunge-17-as-readers-return-to-print.

Reason 4: To Switch Off—Fully!

In our modern connected world, no one really "does nothing" any more. Look around you next time you're waiting for a bus or a plane or standing at an ATM. How many people are doing nothing? My guess is that 80 percent will be on their phone. As smartphone users, the challenge is we're neither focusing fully nor allowing our minds to rest. Both states are compromised. The alarming attention state is simultaneously the least productive and the least relaxing mode (apart from when there really is an emergency, a real wolf at the door rather than what usually is a sheep in wolf's clothing). But doing nothing, letting our minds wander, is pretty much essential if we're to harness our creativity.

"Doing nothing" is also essential in between periods of absorbing or memorizing information. German psychologist Georg Elias Müller and his student Alfons Pilzecker first discovered this in 1900. In one of their many experiments on memory consolidation, Müller and Pilzecker first asked their participants to learn a list of meaningless syllables. Following a short study period, half the group was immediately given a second list to learn while the rest were given a six-minute break before continuing. When tested one-and-a-half hours later, the groups showed strikingly different patterns of recall. The participants given the break remembered nearly 50 percent of their list, compared to an average of 28 percent for the group who had been given no time to recharge their mental batteries. The findings suggest that our ability to memorize new information is especially fragile just after it has first been encoded, making it more susceptible to disruption from new information.

Many further studies carried out over the past century support these findings. We have never had so many distractions to potentially disturb our memory function. Imagine you're a student taking a study break or you are taking a break in the midst of trying to assimilate new information. What are you most likely to pick up first? It'll most likely be your smartphone through which you'll be bombarded with news alerts, messages from friends, new dating matches, eBay wins. Our brains never really get a break as our smartphones lead us straight into alarming mode.

Mind Wandering

Mind wandering was first written about in the 1960s. While similar to the alarming state as both are passive and can take us away from the task at hand, mind wandering can play a vital role in promoting our creativity. In *The Organized Mind*, Daniel Levitin describes it as "this distinctive and special brain state marked by the flow of connections among disparate ideas and thoughts, and a relative lack of barriers between senses and concepts."[37]

Executive attention and mind wandering can work in tandem a bit like our eyes do. When we are focused on sights near to us, we need to intermittently also look at things far in the distance to protect against eye strain and promote good vision. Quite literally, we need to change our perspective. And so it is with the brain. After concentrating intensely on one problem or one area of learning that takes up our executive functioning, our mind needs to do the opposite, to go on a little ramble, not getting fixated on any one thing but to graze in a fertile and boundaryless pasture.

Many of my clients come to me as individuals or couples when their executive decision-making has failed. They've brought their intellect to bear on their issue, let's say, to stay in a job or to leave, to remain in a relationship or break up. They're so close to the issue that there's a need for their minds to zoom out, wander, and look for new associations for old problems. In short, it requires creative, new ways of thinking.

Unfortunately, for many, letting the mind wander in wild pastures can be a fast track to anxiety. One client of mine, explaining why she always has music playing—even when she sleeps—said: "I don't want random thoughts cropping up."

For those who are very anxious, mind wandering can lead down a dark Google rabbit hole with hyperlinks to even darker chambers. A harmless thought such as "Oh, I've got that pain in my knee back again, I must book a doctor's appointment" could lead to "Maybe I have cancer?" and a smartphone Google search for bone cancer within seconds. Obviously these thoughts are unlikely to fuel our creative fire. So how can we harness our mind wandering to serve rather than stress us?

Our minds are like dogs (or at least like my dog!). When trained they can be our best allies, but untrained they can be extremely destructive. I had this experience firsthand with my dog, Madra, a retired racing greyhound. The first couple of weeks after I adopted him were a nightmare. His recall was nonexistent and he tried to attack several small dogs he mistook for rabbits. Allowing him to roam freely was clearly neither advisable nor safe for him or any small dogs in the vicinity. However, 18 months later I can trust him to be off leash to

---

37   Levitin, *The Organized Mind*, 38.

wander, sniff, and discover new things. It took a year of patient training, working on recall and socialization, to get us to this point.

Our minds are also trainable (remember the section on neuroplasticity?). In the first chapter I shared with you that the amount of time needed to change a habit is anywhere between 21 and 66 days. Unfortunately, many of us give up prematurely as we're so impatient to see the fruits of our behavioral change labor. The new neural pathways or "ski runs" still feel lumpy, bumpy, and energy-consuming to go down, so we feel drawn back to the flattened, well-worn tracks that we know from years or even decades of descent. Patience and endurance are key if we are to lay down those new tracks.

On Meditation

Meditation is one of the most effective tools I know in retraining the mind. As an antidote to anxiety, distraction, lack of focus, poor memory, brain aging, and depression, it would be hard to find a rival to meditation. It's even been found to stimulate creativity. A vast amount of research backs this up. Just to give you some examples, research carried out at Harvard University in 2011 found that an eight-week Mindfulness-Based Stress Reduction (MBSR) program increased gray matter concentration in the hippocampus, which governs learning and memory, and in certain areas of the brain that affect emotion regulation and processing. There were also *decreases* in brain cell volume in the amygdala, which controls fear, anxiety, and stress. The scans were backed up by anecdotes from the participants, who said they felt less stressed and happier overall.[38] Another study found that just a *couple* of weeks of meditation training helped people's focus and memory during the verbal reasoning section of the GRE (a standardized test that is required to be taken by students applying to US graduate schools). The impact on their scores was estimated to be equivalent to 16 percentile points.[39]

A growing number of studies have also shown that, given its effects on the self-control regions of the brain, meditation can be very effective in helping people recover from various types of addiction. One study, for example, compared the effectiveness of mindfulness training against the American Lung Association's Freedom From Smoking (FFS) program

---

38 B. K. Hölzel, et al., "Mindfulness Practice Leads to Increases in Regional Brain Gray Matter Density," *Psychiatry Research*, vol. 191, no. 1 (2010): 36–43. doi:10.1016/j.pscychresns.2010.08.006.

39 M. D. Mrazek, et al., "Mindfulness Training Improves Working Memory Capacity and GRE Performance While Reducing Mind Wandering," *Psychological Science*, vol. 24, no. 5 (2013): 776–781. doi.org/10.1177/0956797612459659.

and found that people who learned mindfulness were many times more likely to have quit smoking by the end of the training, and at the 17-week follow-up point, than those in the conventional treatment.[40] The practice of meditation trains us to not hop aboard our cravings but allows more of a gap between trigger and response. In this way, it could potentially also help us not succumb to the lure of our smartphone every time we feel a craving to check it.

When I explore meditation as a potential coping mechanism with clients, I'll often be greeted with "Oh, I cannot not think" or "I've tried but I cannot shut down the thoughts." Many are turned off by the idea that we need to sit down cross-legged, quietly and thoughtlessly, for 15 minutes. For our Western bodies and minds this is pretty much like proposing to someone who has never run before to start training for a marathon with "just" a five-mile run. I'd imagine if they tried that, they'd probably never run again!

In the exercises that follow, I provide some tips on how to get started with meditation, if you've never tried it before. I also make some other suggestions on how to train your executive function, nurture your creativity, create the conditions for safe mind wandering, and perhaps most challenging of all, help you to switch off.

---

40   J. A. Brewer, et al., "Mindfulness Training for Smoking Cessation: Results from a Randomized Controlled Trial," *Drug and Alcohol Dependence*, vol. 119, no. 1–2 (2011): 72–80. doi.org/10.1016/j.drugalcdep.2011.05.027.

···················· **EXERCISES** ····················

Phone Usage Patterns (PUP)   **Week 4**

	Mon	Tue	Wed	Thu	Fri	Sat	Sun
Total estimated time							
Messaging, texting							
Calls							
Browsing							
Shopping							
Dating							
Facebook							
Instagram							
Twitter							
Porn							
Netflix, Amazon Prime, YouTube							
Gaming							
Other							

	Mon	Tue	Wed	Thu	Fri	Sat	Sun
Wait training: Note your phone-free activities or periods that you went without your phone.							

What were the feelings that came up today?

Monday: _____

_____

Tuesday: _____

_____

Wednesday: _____

_____

Thursday: _____

_____

Friday: _____

_____

Saturday: _____

_____

Sunday: _____

_____

* * *

1. What did you try to reduce your phone use this week? Detail it here and rate its effectiveness on a scale of 0 to 10 (0 is totally useless, had no effect; 10 is totally effective).

_____

_____

_____

_____

_____

2. Try Pomodoro/OHIO!

The Pomodoro/OHIO techniques can be applied to almost anything. Start with a task that isn't too cumbersome. It might be to pay all your outstanding bills or address your email backlog. It's about fencing off blocks of time for specific things to wean you off hopping back and forth between activities.

Some OHIO suggestions:

❑ Respond to outstanding email.

❑ Clean out the refrigerator.

❑ File your old bills.

❑ Empty your laundry basket and finally hand wash those delicates that have been lurking at the bottom!

❑ File your tax return or gather all the scattered documents you need in order to file it (in my experience a more time-consuming task!).

Write down one task that you've been struggling to complete that you could try out the Pomodoro/OHIO technique on.

_____

3. Get in nature.

As humans become more urbanized, we increasingly lose touch with nature, our bodies falling out of sync with the seasons, flora, and fauna. The attention restoration theory (ART), which is backed up by much scientific research, asserts that simply spending time in nature can make us more attentive and perceptive. There are well-documented physical health benefits too. "Within 15 minutes of being in nature, your stress level goes down, your heart rate, blood pressure improves," said Dr. Nooshin Razani, a pediatrician and nature researcher with UCSF Benioff Children's Hospital Oakland.[41] The capacity for nature to restore us has been recognized by the National Health Service in the UK, with general practitioners on the Shetland Islands now prescribing outdoor activities such as bird watching, shell gathering, and hiking for many illnesses including anxiety and depression.

I live in a densely populated city yet even here it's possible to find pockets of thriving natural environments. About a year ago I stopped looking at my phone during breaks between clients, instead using the time to roam around a local park. I was much more clear-headed and quite simply more attentive when I'd see a client after a stroll in the park versus after spending the same amount of time scrolling through my phone.

When was the last time you took a walk through a forest or by the ocean, or even in a local park? I will often question a client who is feeling anxious or has bad insomnia about how much time they spend outdoors in nature. Many struggle to remember when they last had a walk in a natural environment. Or perhaps they do walk through parks en route to work but aren't taking the environment in. This was brought home to me when a client who had lost her smartphone named one of the benefits of being without her phone as noticing nature a lot more on her route to work. She said she felt a lot more relaxed starting her day as a result.

A common excuse is "I don't have enough time." I work with clients to gently challenge their perceptions, looking at how they use their lunch times or how they can siphon off time from their commute to walk a bit of their journey, getting off a stop early to walk through a small garden square, even. It's amazing the difference it can make.

---

41   John Tara, "Doctors Are Prescribing Nature to Patients in the UK's Shetland Islands," *CNN Health*, October 5, 2018, https://edition .cnn.com/2018/10/05/health/nature-prescriptions-shetland-intl/index.html.

Think of a natural environment you walk through regularly. It could be by a river, a stream, a small park, or a beach. Choose one of those locations and describe it here—the sights, sounds, and smells you remember from that place.

_____

_____

_____

_____

_____

Next time you go there, switch your phone and any music-playing devices off! Look around you, notice what you see, what you hear. And when you come back, write it down here.

_____

_____

_____

_____

_____

Is there a difference? Do you notice more, sense more, or feel more without your phone or other digital device?

_____

_____

_____

_____

_____

4. Meditate

Anyone can meditate. All it requires is breath, something all of us living beings are blessed with. Here's how to get started:

❏ Create a dedicated space, perhaps with a nice candle or some incense (but only if that works for you) in a corner of your home that feels safe and peaceful.

❏ Sit on the floor, cross-legged if possible, but any reasonably comfortable seated position will do.

❏ Start small. Set your alarm for one minute, sit down, close your eyes, and just focus on your breath, taking long deep breaths in and out, creating some stillness within yourself. When you get distracted, just keep focusing on the breath, letting the thoughts just drift by you.

❏ Once you feel comfortable meditating for a minute then try lengthening it to 90 seconds and then to two minutes, and continue until you've reached a duration that you feel content with and can manage to fit into your daily routine (this is crucial!).

The most important thing is to manage your expectations! Many meditation novices feel like they have to sit for 20 to 30 minutes or there's no point. They then feel discouraged when they cannot accomplish this and just give up. Someone once described the practice of meditation as like sitting at a train station letting the trains go past, not boarding any particular train, but equally not pretending they're not there, not trying to stop or obstruct them (a pretty bad idea!), and not trying to follow them to the end of the line.

Many of my clients find meditation apps useful. I have some reservations about them as they can create a further level of dependency on our smartphones, but, used carefully, they may be helpful for some. If you find one you like, I'd encourage you to download it so you can at least put your device in airplane mode when you're using it. Otherwise, a great, simple book on mindfulness is *Moment by Moment* by Jerry Braza. It's out of print but can be easily found secondhand online.

5. Engage your creativity.

Whether it's painting, cooking, writing, drawing, improvisation, or picking up a musical instrument, find something that channels your creativity. I could write another book on the joy many of my clients have found through reengaging with long-abandoned creative pursuits. Our creativity is very vulnerable and, unfortunately for many of us, has been wounded through having received messages about not being "the creative type" from teachers or parents.

If you still feel inhibited, here are some suggestions:

❑ Borrow or buy the book *The Artist's Way*, a fantastic guide to clearing away the blocks that stop us from being creative. Make sure it's a hard copy—remember texts we read offline are more likely to be assimilated and remembered.

❑ Join a Meetup group (www.meetup.com) that focuses on creativity. There are several that follow *The Artist's Way* workbook, but there are many others focusing on specific creative pursuits. People join these groups as they typically find more synergy when collaborating with others and being accountable to others than when working individually. If that's you too then I'd strongly urge you to give it a go!

❑ Contact local adult education colleges to see what they offer. I found my very reasonably priced painting course through a local city-run institution. There's a surprising amount of low-cost ongoing education options available in most towns and cities.

6. Schedule time for mind wandering.

When traveling by train or bus, I always allocate some time to do absolutely nothing, besides the obvious smartphone switch-off; it also means no book, no magazines, nothing concrete to focus my attention on. There are many opportunities for this—when traveling, waiting at the ATM, for an Uber pickup, any time you might find yourself reaching for your phone, don't. Just do nothing. This may sound easy but for many of us it's these times that we feel most bored or most vulnerable. Many people feel extremely uncomfortable and exposed when they're alone waiting for a friend/partner, and a phone can lessen those feelings as we make ourselves look busy.

Challenge yourself to commit to not reaching for your phone when you feel that itch. Note here how you feel and where your mind wanders to.

_____

_____

_____

_____

_____

CHAPTER 5

Tackling Boredom and Emotional Discomfort

"All of humanity's problems stem from man's
inability to sit quietly in a room alone."

—Pascal

Anxiety is probably the most common presenting issue among my client base. One of my clients stands out as having a particularly long history of it; she doesn't remember a time when anxiety wasn't a feature of her life. Over the years I've worked with her, she has gained a lot of understanding as to what lies behind her anxiety to the extent that it no longer derails her. Though still prone to anxiety in certain situations, like most of us, her baseline state is a lot calmer. In the initial stages of our work together, I would try and get her to imagine what life without anxiety might look like, how she might feel in its absence. She confessed that one of her fears was that once the anxiety faded away, boredom would loom large in the foreground. Over her decades-long acquaintance with anxiety, she knew and had become accustomed to it, but boredom inspired a real sense of dread in her.

Sure enough, as her anxiety lessened, boredom did start to make its presence felt in her life. However, over time, my client came to embrace this new state. She labeled it "a privilege" and a sign that anxiety had released its stranglehold over her life. Interestingly, when she stopped reacting to and judging her boredom, it started to ease. Different things came to occupy the void previously occupied by her anxiety and fear. She started writing and engaging in creative pursuits again. For this client, boredom was the vacuum left by her anxiety. Perhaps her case is not that unusual. German philosopher Arthur Schopenhauer asserted that as humans we are "doomed to vacillate between the two extremities of distress and boredom."[42] Boredom and anxiety are curious bedfellows. On the surface, they have little in common. The former suggests disengagement, a lack of arousal. Anxiety, on the other hand, is denoted by alertness, our antennae up and monitoring for potential threat or danger. But both are uncomfortable states for many of us.

My client's attitude toward boredom taught me a lot. It led me to reflect upon the taboo around boredom. Many of us will gladly profess to be busy and stressed as these states confer a sense of industriousness and purpose, suggest that we're important, we're needed! But boredom? Broadly speaking, it's not perceived as a particularly adult emotion. In spite of this a recent Gallup poll found that 70 percent of Americans find their work boring.[43] Considering that the average American spends an estimated 40 hours per week at work, that's a lot of bored Americans!

Much consumer marketing, advertising, and product development is designed to address boredom. Indeed, if we were more comfortable being bored or sufficiently creative to amuse ourselves without the aid of consumer goods, then our capitalist society would probably collapse. Some advertising explicitly pitches to bored consumers. In a recent search for a tablet computer, I read in one product blurb that with the purchase of said device one "need never be bored again."

People will go to great lengths to escape boredom. Many of us would rather feel pain or discomfort than nothing at all. In 2014, Harvard psychologists found that faced with spending 15 minutes alone in a room with no stimulation (read: no smartphone!), two-thirds of men pressed a button in the knowledge that it would deliver a painful jolt. One man found being left alone in his own company so disagreeable he opted to be shocked 190 times. Under the same conditions, a quarter of women pressed the shock button. The scientists attributed the difference in self-shocking levels between the men and women to the fact that men

---

42   Viktor Frankl, *The Unheard Cry for Meaning: Psychotherapy and Humanism* (New York: Simon and Schuster, 1978).

43   Amy Adkins, "Majority of US Employees Not Engaged Despite Gains in 2014," *Gallup,* January 28, 2015, https://news.gallup.com/poll/181289/majority-employees-not-engaged-despite-gains-2014.aspx.

tend to be more sensation-seeking. Timothy Wilson, who led the research, attributed the findings to humans' "constant urge to do something rather than nothing."[44]

For many of us, boredom can feel like nothingness, a void where we're not feeling much, not doing much. As a child, probably the worst thing I could say to my mom was "I'm bored." I was looking for a solution to this dilemma, something to do, some entertainment. Maybe children no longer get bored, or if they do, perhaps they're pawned off with a parent's smartphone. As adults we've learned to digitally self-soothe, pulling out our smartphones for pretty much the same reason people might have lit up a cigarette a few decades ago: something to kill time with. Our smartphones are the ultimate one-stop boredom reliever. No wonder we cannot put them down. We may not admit to being bored but why else can't we go 12 minutes without checking our devices? If being glued to one's smartphone can be taken as a gauge of boredom levels, it seems a lot of us are bored a lot of the time!

Boredom and Addiction

"The truth is, many people fall into drug and alcohol addiction because of boredom. It's something to do." I read this on the website of Raleigh House, a rehab center in Colorado, recently. I believe the same principle applies to our smartphone addictions. Being constantly on our phones keeps boredom at bay.

The second chapter of this workbook addressed the addictive qualities of smartphones in general, and how we get hooked. Several key features of our smartphones can be very magnetic to the bored mind. Take, for instance, messaging (including texting, WhatsApp, Telegram, etc.), which remains the most popular smartphone function.[45] We expect replies more quickly than ever before. When email was introduced, traditional mail was dubbed "snail mail." Now email has been consigned to the same category. On our chat apps we can see if the recipient has read our message and whether they're replying in real time or not. Natasha Dow Schüll, a cultural anthropologist who has researched gambling addiction, likens "the roller-coaster ride of texting" to playing slot machines. Quoted in a *Financial Times* article on modern dating, she compares leaving a message on an answering machine to buying a lottery ticket because you don't expect an immediate payoff. But texting taps

44   Ian Sample, "Shocking But True: Students Prefer Jolt of Pain to Being Made to Sit and Think," *The Guardian*, July 3, 2014, https://www.theguardian.com/science/2014/jul/03/electric-shock-preferable-to-thinking-says-study.

45   Statista, "What Functions/Apps on Your Smartphone Do You Use Most Frequently?" accessed January 12, 2019, https://www.statista.com/statistics/713927/smartphone-functions-and-apps-used-most-frequently-in-the-us.

into what Schüll dubs the "ludic loop" of the slot-machine experience.[46] "The possibility of instant gratification coupled with reward uncertainty draws us into the game, and the absence of built-in stopping mechanisms makes us keep playing," she says.[47] These ups and downs, highs and lows, are the antidote to boredom, a roller-coaster ride for our jaded, bored selves.

The human brain produces more dopamine when it anticipates a reward but doesn't know when it will arrive. Most of the alluring apps and websites in wide use today were engineered to exploit this habit-forming loop.[48]

Boredom and Meaninglessness

In an article for *The Atlantic* based on her book *Yawn: Adventures in Boredom*, author Mary Mann says: "It's easier to label that itchy sensation 'boredom' than it is to consider the feeling one gets sometimes that the train of life is stopped on its tracks, that the narrative is going nowhere." She adds, "Because boredom is such a motivating, annoying, irritating force, boredom can be kind of useful."[49]

Existential therapist, neurologist, and Holocaust survivor Viktor Frankl wrote in *Man's Search for Meaning*: "Boredom is now causing more problems to solve than distress. And these problems are growing increasingly crucial, for progressive automation will probably lead to an enormous increase in the leisure hours available to the average worker. The pity of it is that many of these will not know what to do with all their newly acquired free time." Frankl wrote his book half a century before the invention of the smartphone and obviously hadn't reckoned on a portable device that would act as a gateway to every possible type of entertainment! Frankl asserted that in the post-war years, the mass of people living lives without meaning led to the rise of what he termed the "mass neurotic triad"—namely depression, aggression, and addiction.

---

46 *Financial Times*, "Love and Texts: Seduction in the Digital Age," July 20,2018, https://www.ft.com/content/51c350da-8a19-11e8-bf9e -8771d5404543.

47 *Financial Times*, "Love and Texts: Seduction in the Digital Age."

48 *Time*, "You're Addicted to Your Smartphone. This Company Thinks It Can Change That," April 13, 2018, http://time.com/5237434/ youre-addicted-to-your-smartphone-this-company-thinks-it-can-change-that.

49 Julie Beck, "The Virtues of Boredom," *The Atlantic*, May 8, 2017, https://www.theatlantic.com/health/archive/2017/05/ the-virtues-of-boredom/525642.

The human brain produces more dopamine when it anticipates a reward but doesn't know when it will arrive. Most of the alluring apps and websites in wide use today were engineered to exploit this habit-forming loop.

Frankl was imprisoned in the Dachau concentration camp for one-and-a-half years. "Distressing" seems a gross understatement to describe what he lived through. But rather than focus on this traumatic experience, what he was drawn to amid the environment of loss and despair was the role finding a sense of meaning played in his survival. In the bleakness of Dachau he was able to find something of value within himself that he could connect with, namely, the love he felt for his wife. The acknowledgment of this love acted like a touchstone for Frankl and gave him the power and sense of purpose he needed to survive.

Frankl's belief was that no matter what life serves up, if one takes appropriate action and adopts the right attitude to the situation, a meaningful existence can be realized. His experience of transcending the conditions of Dachau would certainly attest to this. To extrapolate Frankl's philosophy, the antidote to boredom and boredom-induced addiction is to find a meaning, a sense of purpose to our lives. If we have that we are insulated from the "What does it matter, why should I bother?" despondency that is the breeding ground for boredom and also addiction.

Many of us need to go through years of doing things that feel unimportant, unstimulating—in short, boring—until we can bear no more and are pushed to develop a sense of what we were put on this Earth to do. That was certainly my experience. For half a decade I plodded along in a fog knowing that I wasn't fulfilled in my career. I was making just enough effort to keep my slate clean and my boss off my back. I felt stuck but lacked the energy required to make the jump to something else. I had an aptitude for what I was doing, which allowed me to coast, a particularly deadening state for me. I had my epiphany moment in the middle of a conference on some hard-core technology in Washington. The fact that I didn't understand what was being discussed was the least of my worries. I felt I was in the wrong place. I had no business being there.

This was 15 years ago, well before the iPhone hit Apple store shelves. If I had a smartphone then I might not have had this moment of realization and failed to hear the internal voice screaming, "Get the hell out of this job, this career. Do something, do anything, but don't do this!" Instead, I would have been busy distracting myself, messaging my friends, perhaps even watching something on YouTube, putting off the inevitable point when I would finally have said, "Enough, no more."

Listen to Your Boredom—It Might Have Something to Tell You

When I work with boredom, I take a similar approach as when addressing anxiety. Rather than reacting to it, trying to suppress it, distract from it, I encourage my clients to treat it with curiosity (curiosity being another natural antidote to boredom!). Being bored, feeling unstimulated is certainly part of the ebb and flow of life, and if we go with it rather than distract ourselves from it, we can learn a lot about being still and patient.

But there are times when prolonged enduring boredom can be a signal that we're not using our skills and talents, we're not channeling our creativity. In short, that we've stalled and have become stuck, like I was at the tech conference.

Like anxiety, this brand of enduring, persistent boredom underpinned by a sense that one's contribution doesn't make a difference can be a powerful catalyst for change when faced without judgment. Ask yourself, what is boredom trying to tell you? Mine was like a hacked, belligerent GPS shouting, "Stop! This is a dead end. Turn around and go back. Find another route!" Listening to that voice formed the first step in embarking on a career that I find very fulfilling. Had I not had that intense moment of boredom at the tech conference and felt my body, soul, and mind's strong reaction to it, I doubt I'd now be a qualified therapist writing this book.

Embrace the Void

You've now passed the halfway point of this book. Hopefully, you've noticed your phone use dipping. Maybe you feel bored and you don't know what to do with the free time you've created; welcome to "the void." This is a good place to be.

Before I was asked to write this book—in fact, the night before I was approached by the publisher—I was running a bath and reflecting that I didn't have much work going on and maybe I was starting to feel a little bored. If you're self-employed, perhaps you can relate. Sometimes you feel too busy, sometimes you feel like you're underworked. Moments when work is just enough seem rare! I reflected on having half the number of clients I had six months before. While I wasn't in financial jeopardy, that thought alone could have triggered some anxiety. But I caught myself, telling myself, "Enjoy this time because it won't last." The next day I received an email asking me to write a book on phone addiction. Of course, things don't always happen as neatly as that. But had I been rushing to fill the void of a half-empty client calendar the previous month, perhaps I would have had to turn down this opportunity.

Suppressed Emotions and Addiction

Most of my clients will come to therapy at the point when their previous coping mechanisms have failed. It could be that they're burnt out, they can no longer sustain 50-hour work weeks, or they're partied out, their bodies can no longer do it. Overconsumption of alcohol, work, porn, streamed TV series, drugs, or gambling all serve the same purpose ultimately—to keep feelings at bay.

Smartphone use is invariably part of the cocktail but never the presenting factor (at least to date). The word I hear most often in connection with smartphones is "distraction," and yes, they can be incredibly distracting buzzing, flashing, bleeping, ringing little things. But when my clients describe their devices in this way, they're invariably referring to them as distractions from work, proper conversations with friends, exercise, tackling something they've been putting off. However, the really sticky lure of smartphones, which is usually not made conscious, is their power to distract us from pain or any other unwanted emotion, how they serve to numb us, at least temporarily.

When starting work with clients in therapy, the situation initially can often feel for worse before it becomes better. I believe this is because clients typically embark on therapy with a dam of suppressed emotions that is near breaking point. That tide of emotion is being held back by the suppression tactics listed above. As the client's attachment to those coping mechanisms becomes gently loosened, emotion floods through. That's certainly been my experience of successful therapy. What's suppressed needs to surface so that it can be worked through and healed.

If a person's coping mechanism is particularly harmful—a substance addiction or gambling habit—it is generally easier to identify and they will typically be forced to confront it by family, friends, or their employer. Smartphone addiction is so much more insidious.

Socially sanctioned and ubiquitous, it's much harder to detect, rarely getting to the breaking point most of us need to feel before we look for help.

In a brilliant *Harvard Business Review* article on the ways we avoid unwanted feelings, author Charlotte Lieberman eloquently shares her pattern of "mindlessly" reaching for her phone in an attempt to muffle uncomfortable emotions. She states, "The distraction afforded by constant connection to social media, news, email, and texting may feel comforting in the short term, but in the long term it may sap what poet John Berryman referred to as 'inner resources.' In enabling us to avoid ourselves, our phones allow us to look away from anxious feelings instead of trying to resolve them."[50]

A client of mine once described how she spent her late twenties feeling very lonely and uncomfortable in her state of singledom. Being single had come as a jolt for her after being in relationships for her entire adult life. I asked how she managed to cope with those feelings. She explained that she had discovered Netflix and spent her weekends watching series in marathon sessions. "I simply no longer had any time to feel lonely," she said.

Interestingly, this client entered therapy when she had finally found the solid relationship she was looking for. But, ultimately, the questions she had temporarily quashed by her Netflix habit kept springing up. She came to learn that it wasn't simply being single that she found challenging, it was getting to know herself, discovering what her purpose was. Her female identity had previously been very much tied up with having a partner, and being single signaled a loss of self-esteem. This belief was difficult to dismantle as it was instilled in her from a very young age. Finding herself suddenly single at an age she felt she should be settling down shook the foundation of her self-confidence. She viewed the state of singledom as an indication that she wasn't sufficiently interesting, intelligent, or desirable for a man to want to commit to. Attempting to answer some of those questions took a good six months of therapy, during which she got to question the wholesale values that had been passed down to her by her parents and gain a better knowledge of herself and what made her happy. This required some bravery; it also necessitated disengaging the soothing drip feed of Netflix.

In enabling us to avoid ourselves, our phones allow us to look away
from anxious feelings instead of trying to resolve them.

---

50   Charlotte Lieberman, "What You're Hiding from When You Constantly Check Your Phone," *Harvard Business Review*, January 19, 2016, https://hbr.org/2016/01/what-youre-hiding-from-when-you-constantly-check-your-phone.

Speaking of Netflix, CEO Reed Hastings named the streaming service's main competitor as sleep rather than what you might imagine it to be—Amazon Prime Video or YouTube. In a way, that actually makes a lot of sense but it's also quite a superficial take on what excessive Netflix consumption is costing us. Sleep, of course, is vital for our well-being and health, but so are self-awareness and paying attention to where we are in our lives, and asking those searching questions of ourselves, which many of us quash or put off answering through binge consumption of TV series. But we ignore those difficult questions at our peril, and risk sleepwalking through life, glassy-eyed and empty, wishing away the multiple 15-second periods 'til the next episode loads.

In the words of the poet Robert Frost, "the only way out is through." Even our most painful emotions give us valuable insights as to who we are, how we relate to those around us, what makes us tick. We pay a high price for our avoidance of both emotional discomfort and boredom, whether it's via the pacifier of our smartphones, alcohol, drugs, shopping, or gambling.

Being able to recognize and handle our emotions is the true barometer of our emotional health. Unfortunately not many of us have had this modeled to us growing up. It's no surprise that as a practicing therapist I would recommend my own profession as a way of learning healthier methods of identifying and managing our emotions. However, I've felt the benefit of therapy in my own life as it's helped me identify the reasons behind my own sense of lethargy and inaction, and ultimately change that.

There is a perception that therapy is a costly pursuit, a privilege of the middle and upper classes, and indeed it can be with many experienced therapists charging upward of £70/$130 per session. But there are many ways to access therapy. While I was training—and indeed for two years after I qualified—I volunteered at a wonderful low-cost counseling center run as a charity, Help Counselling, in London's Notting Hill. Clients there paid anything between £5 and £30 (about $7 and $40) per session depending on what they earned. Most accredited therapy-training institutions insist that their graduates have at least 200 hours of therapy work under their belts to graduate. So if you live in a metropolitan area there's a good chance you can access low-cost therapy in this way. A good place to start is by contacting therapy-training institutions. If you're not in a city, there's always the possibility of Skype sessions from some of these institutions.

Another key benefit of therapy (and meditation too, I should add) is to make us more attentive to the hints we receive in life as to what is meaningful for us, what gives us a sense of purpose. I recently worked with a client who was considering reentering the workforce in either a paid or volunteer capacity. We worked on trying to dismantle some of her fears around what it might be like to work again after 15 years off, what that work might be, and where her interests now lay. On a summer vacation with her family, my client came across a stray dog, which she and her kids took care of for the duration of their stay. As the vacation drew to an end she was determined not to leave the dog behind to a sure fate of local dog catchers and a kill shelter. Using her resourcefulness and determination she found a way to ship the dog back to the UK and to a new life.

She returned to therapy after that vacation with a new sense of purpose to get more involved in dog rescue. While therapy had raised many questions about feeling unfulfilled and frustrated that she wasn't channeling her skills and following her passions, it had also led to her being awake and alert to a sense of possibility that her questions were being answered in the shape of a stray unwanted dog.

EXERCISES

Phone Usage Patterns (PUP)   **Week 5**

	Mon	Tue	Wed	Thu	Fri	Sat	Sun
Total estimated time							
Messaging, texting							
Calls							
Browsing							
Shopping							
Dating							
Facebook							
Instagram							
Twitter							
Porn							
Netflix, Amazon Prime, YouTube							
Gaming							
Other							

	Mon	Tue	Wed	Thu	Fri	Sat	Sun
Wait training: Note your phone-free activities or periods that you went without your phone.							

What were the feelings that came up today?

Monday:
_____

_____

Tuesday:
_____

_____

Wednesday:
_____

_____

Thursday:
_____

_____

Friday:
_____

_____

Saturday:
_____

_____

Sunday:
_____

_____

* * *

1. What did you try to reduce your phone use this week? Detail it here and rate its effectiveness on a scale of 0 to 10 (0 is totally useless, had no effect; 10 is totally effective).

_____

_____

_____

_____

_____

2. Review

We're now at roughly the midway point of this workbook. Look back over your phone usage. Are you noticing any patterns over the past few weeks? Are you using your phone on days where you're feeling more anxious, sad, bored? What are you avoiding?

_____

_____

_____

_____

Is there another way you can express those emotions rather than scrolling on your phone?

_____

_____

_____

_____

Many of us lug around so many silent frustrations, whether it's with our boss, our friend, our partner, or our roommate. Our phones can act like pacifiers. They shut us up, contain us, but as adults that's not always a mature, sustainable approach to managing our feelings. Is there stuff that you feel has been left unexpressed on the days when your phone usage is high?

_____

_____

_____

_____

_____

3. Find a sense of meaning.

Write a letter to yourself, imagining you're 80 (if you're 80, imagine you're 95!). With those extra years of life experience, what have you learned? What will you consider to be most important? We all have within us the seeds of maturity, ready to shoot if we pay attention.

A good time to do this exercise would be after meditation (see page 66) or after a walk in nature. Find a quiet time and a quiet place for your letter writing. From the vantage point of your imagined 80-year-old wiser self, look back at the younger version of yourself—you now. What advice would you give yourself as to what's important, what you should focus on, what your purpose is? Address it like a real letter. You can put your future address down (where you'd like to be living at that point!).

Read your letter carefully after you've written it, and really take it in. Keep it safe, and, when you feel directionless, refer to it as your guide.

On another day, go through the same process as above, but this time, imagine you're eight years old. Sometimes it helps to look at an old picture to remind yourself of what you looked like at that age, your hobbies, your friends, your pets, and what your world was like. Some find this exercise easier than the other one because all readers of this book will have been eight already! At eight years old, most of us were following our passions and found a way to engage with them as often as possible or as much as our parents/teachers permitted! So from that mindset, what would your eight-year-old self remind you of? What would they tell you to do less or more of?

Circle the points you really want to incorporate from the two letters and commit to something you can do right now, some change you can make, big or small, though I would urge you to start with the small stuff.

date: _____

Dear 80-year-old self,

date: _____

Dear 8-year-old self,

4. Be open to hints.

What are the questions, uncertainties, and fears that are arising in you as you spend less time on your phone? You may not have the answers yet, but without the questions and the curiosity you cannot start to be open for the answers.

_____

_____

_____

_____

_____

CHAPTER 6

Procrastination: Why We Really Put Stuff Off!

"Until you value yourself, you won't value your time. Until you value your time, you will not do anything with it."

—M. Scott Peck, author of *The Road Less Traveled*

Like boredom and wanting to escape our feelings, procrastination is nothing new. Greek orator Demosthenes allegedly used to shave one side of his head to remain indoors practicing his speeches rather than procrastinating outdoors! When faced with a deadline, *Les Misérables* author Victor Hugo asked his valet to hide his clothes to ensure that he'd stay inside writing. The desire to put off tasks that we don't enjoy is innate in us as humans, but modern life offers us more plentiful distractions than were available to Hugo or Demosthenes. For them, entertainment, news, chatting with friends/acquaintances typically lay outside the home so by remaining indoors there was nothing to do but work. We, however, no longer even need to leave our bedrooms for shopping, entertainment, news, games, or to meet a new partner!

According to Dr. Piers Steel, author of *The Procrastination Equation*, we're "entering the golden age of procrastination." A Distinguished Research Chair at the University of Calgary, where he teaches human resources and organizational dynamics at the Haskayne School of Business, Steel asserts that in the past 40 years there's been about a 300 to 400 percent growth in chronic procrastination. Is it a coincidence that this period of upswing coincides with the widespread adoption of TV in the West? If a similar study were to be conducted on chronic procrastination since 2007 (the launch of the iPhone), I wonder how much more dramatic the increase would be.

Steel conducted a series of projects to improve the measurement of procrastination, identify the typical procrastinator, and define effective self-regulatory techniques to prevent procrastination. According to his research, "one in four [people] would describe themselves as a chronic procrastinator, [while] over half the population would describe themselves as frequent."[51] Steel went so far as to draw up an equation to define the probability that we will procrastinate any given task. It looks like this as conceptualized by Daniel J. Levitin in *The Organized Mind*:

$$\text{Procrastination} = \frac{\text{Time to complete task} \times \text{Distractibility}}{\text{Self-confidence} \times \text{Task value}}$$

Mathematical formulas freak a lot of us out. But in a nutshell, Steel asserts that if what's above the line (length of time the task will take x our distractibility) outweighs what's beneath (our self-confidence x the value attached to the task), it's likely that we will procrastinate. If the former significantly outweighs the latter, then maybe we'll never even attempt the task. Let's take a look at each of the elements in what Steel identifies as crucial in governing whether we procrastinate upon a given task or not.

1. Distractibility

As mentioned above, there's nothing new about humans being drawn to distractions. But I'd argue that never before in human civilization have we had so many distractions available in a totally portable device 24/7. According to research carried out in 2014 by Zogby Analytics, for 87 percent of millennials, their smartphones never leave their side. It's not difficult to imagine how, for them, focusing on important but maybe less critically urgent tasks has become increasingly difficult.[52]

51   Tom Heyden, "The Much-Delayed War on Procrastination," *BBC News Magazine*, October 11, 2014, https://www.bbc.co.uk/news/magazine-29570615.

52   Lisa Kiplinger, "Millennials LOVE Their Smartphones: Deal With It," *USA Today*, September 27, 2014, https://eu.usatoday.com/story/money/personalfinance/2014/09/27/millennials-love-smartphones-mobile-study/16192777.

When I printed off the first draft of this chapter to review, the 20-something lady at the print shop glanced at the title and said, "Oh I procrastinate *so* much. I have an essay to write and I just cannot sit down to do it." I told her I'm sure she could, maybe she just didn't particularly relish the thought of the amount of work involved. She responded, "No it's not that, it's my phone. I cannot stay off it. Actually I need the screen repaired so I'm hoping that I'll get it written while it's at the Apple Store. I just need it to be taken away." I shared some tips with her on how to manage her phone, including the Chapter 3 tip (page 36) about sticking your phone in another room, switched off, while you write.

2. Time to Complete

On the one hand, there's not much we can do about this one. A task takes as long as it takes. But one thing's for certain—the more distracted we are the more time it will take! Here again, our phones can undermine us. I know if I have my phone on and my Gmail account open I will need to add about 20 percent onto the time estimate to complete any given task. If, on the other hand, I focus on it completely (with phone off and in a different room) I'll be lowering both my capacity for distraction and the time it'll take me. A win-win, in other words!

3. Self-Confidence

Our smartphones can lead us to procrastinate in more subtle ways. Take my writing this book, something which I valued highly but which was likely to take a long time to complete. To be writing a book about phone addiction while having my device on and buzzing would have felt not only counterintuitive but also hypocritical ("Do as I say not as I do."). But it also could have led me down a path that would have severely undermined the confidence I had in my ability to write this book.

When I was commissioned to write it, my first instinct was to see who else has written on this topic and what exactly they'd written. A moment later (before I had entered "phone addiction book" into the Google search box), I stopped myself, pulling back from the cliff edge of creative self-annihilation. Had I googled, I would no doubt have found authors I deemed more erudite, with more letters after their names, and thus, to my mind, better equipped to write such a book. I would perhaps also have come across their glowing reviews, their "NYT best seller" badges, none of which would have helped me get out of the starting blocks with my book. Building on the running analogy, I would have felt a twinge in my knee, my laces would have felt too tight, and hell, I would have been wearing the wrong shoes as well! I would have used whatever reason I could to pull out of the race as I didn't fancy my chances of winning. In short, smartphones can be a gateway for comparison, thus potentially undermining our own confidence in succeeding at whatever task we deem challenging.

It's an issue I come across repeatedly with my clients. Typically, they're about to embark upon something new or outside their comfort zone. It could be a hobby, a creative path, a new job, a new career. But when they start their Google research, they see others that have gotten to it first or done better, been recognized and celebrated. I rate self-confidence as the most important factor in the procrastination equation. Even believing in ourselves as procrastinators can become a self-fulfilling prophesy that undermines our trying new things.

Perfectionism is the arch enemy of self-confidence and is often the procrastinator's biggest challenge. It takes humility to complete something. It's a risk to say it's done when we feel if only we had another hour, another day, another week, another year it could be much better, perfect even.

Self-confidence is about not tying one's self-worth to this one thing, one task. It takes confidence to be able to say what you've done is okay and good as it is, and then to let it go. While also acknowledging it could be better, you let it out into the world because you want to move on and do other things as well as have a balance in your life.

4. Task Value

Procrastination, when it's severe, is rarely just about getting something done. Of course, many of us put off dreaded daily chores—hand washing our delicates, taking out the garbage, or cleaning the windows—but the most serious type of procrastination is that which stops us from getting on with our lives and achieving our goals. Take, for example, someone who wants to change jobs yet puts if off. They may feel the position or place they're in currently is a dead end, yet feel unmotivated to update their resume or contact potential new employers. I see this in many of my clients. To their friends and family it may seem that they are merely procrastinating, yet often, it's more complicated than that. Often what lies beneath their procrastination is fear. It could be fear of success, fear of failure, or both! Interestingly, it's the high-task-value goals that trigger the most deep-rooted fears.

I once worked with a client who wanted to be a professional writer. A talented amateur writer, her dream was to complete and publish a novel. But she put off writing that novel, a task she valued extremely highly, for years, although she had many ideas and no shortage of inspiration. Together we explored what was blocking her from starting her novel. One of the fears at the core of her blockage was that she would invest all her energy into writing a book, submit if for publication, and have it be rejected. That, she felt, would be proof that she actually wasn't that talented. The other fear, which was even greater than the first, was that her book would be accepted for publication and available in book stores for people to read. When I asked what that might feel like, she said "terrifying." A private person by nature, she felt that her writing would expose her to the world. So the task value became something that held her back! For this reason, I feel that Steel's formula needs amending in some cases, because when the perceived value of the task is extremely high, we are more likely to procrastinate on it.

What lies beneath procrastination is fear. It could be fear of success, fear of failure, or both! Interestingly, it's the high task value goals that trigger the most deep-rooted fears.

It sounds counterintuitive, but many of us are subconsciously worried about fulfilling our potential. We are often reacting to messages—whether overt or more subtle—that we have received growing up that people who are successful are full of themselves, arrogant, and selfish, and that leads us to keep our own talents hidden.

In my practice, I find that the first step in overcoming procrastination is to find out what the payoff or benefit is in staying where you are versus progressing. Then, weigh that against the payback you might receive in pursuing your goals. In other words, focus on the true net task value.

In practical terms, this might involve looking at how you might feel if you were stuck in your current situation in six months, one year, or five years' time. Often, just imagining that can trigger you to realize that the price of remaining stuck, continually procrastinating, is too much, which can spur you to take steps to change things. It could also involve chair work, where you move between two chairs. In one chair, voice the part of you that is resistant to change, and then shift to the other chair to speak from the part of yourself that wants a shift. Getting both parts to dialogue can be really helpful as each part gives the other a hearing, and you can respond from both the scared/hesitant side and the brave/forward-moving side. In this way, all of your mixed-up and contradictory voices can get a hearing and be reasoned with.

It could be that part of the potential jobseeker is nervous about starting all over in a new company. But their ego finds it hard to accept that this is part of them because surely, grown-ups shouldn't have such thoughts. So the ego will suppress the real reason for their procrastination from coming to the light. Instead, the jobseeker will find a more acceptable thought, such as, "Now isn't a good time to move. It's very busy. It'll be better next month/next year when I have more time to devote to my search."

By allowing the resistant side full voice, some of a client's more buried fears are allowed to emerge, and the client can start engaging with them. For instance, if a client finally feels safe to admit that starting off somewhere new is a real fear, then the more confident side of them (speaking from the other chair) might suggest something like, "Well, if you do get close to securing a job at the desired company, how about you ask to speak to someone at your level who works there to get an account of their experience and to maybe allay your fear about the new workplace being unfriendly?" When working in this way, I see clients become incredibly creative about finding new ways of managing their fears.

The key really is honesty with oneself, finding out the real reasons behind the procrastination and starting to engage with the obstacles rather than denying their existence. That way, we begin to understand ourselves a bit better instead of kidding ourselves that it's simply that we never get down to things or that we're lazy. The truth is most of us can and will make changes to improve our lives if we take time to understand the real obstacles that block us from moving forward.

Sneaking Up on Procrastination

Proactive Procrastination

Given that most of us procrastinate when faced with tasks with a long completion time, why not accept that and plan for it? When I embarked upon writing this book, it happened to coincide with the start of another project I had to develop more muscle mass in my body, which would help prevent a recurring joint injury. At the time I saw no obvious connection between the two goals. One was mainly an intellectual, creative pursuit and the other a physical one.

It took a frustrating creative block to show me how both tasks could literally feed each other. On one particular day, I had set myself a word count goal but nothing was coming. Previously I might have stayed at my desk, surfed the internet, checked my phone, and chatted on WhatsApp, unmindfully procrastinating and kidding myself that because I was at my computer I was therefore ready for work should the muse alight. The muse was very definitely otherwise occupied that day, and so I made a very deliberate effort to do something different. Also, since I was clocking my internet and phone time, the digital distractions were no longer a valid option anyway! So I went to the gym and had what turned out to be my best workout ever, smashing previous personal bests with apparent ease. I learned that even though it was not an optimum day for my writing it was a good day for me physically! I didn't beat myself up. I still felt like a capable person. That particular day wasn't a productive one for writing, and that was okay. I didn't do any writing for the rest of the day, but nonetheless I felt a sense of achievement and productivity. I didn't feel useless like I had all morning staring at a blank computer screen. I also slept better and woke up the next day very much ready to work. I also had a new idea for my book—proactive procrastination—basically making conscious your desire for distraction and choosing a distraction proactively rather than waiting for your attention to be stolen by whatever sugarcoated digital delight pops up. That way, even if you're not doing the number one important thing on your list, you can prove to yourself that you *can* get some things done.

The Snowball Effect

On a recent holiday I had the good fortune to be totally off grid with no WiFi or cell reception, and it was blissful. I was in Baja California, Mexico, camping on a UNESCO-protected island and learning to free dive with a wonderful organization called I AM WATER (iamwateroceantravel.com), which does much to promote marine conservation globally. It's a sport I had wanted to try for a long time, and I had finally taken some time off work to explore it. I learned a lot about myself while free diving. Relying solely on one's breath-hold and calmness of mind to stay safely underwater, it's more an exercise in mindfulness than it is in athletic ability.

What was interesting, though, was how a week's digital detox resulted in my becoming more spontaneous, more open to other opportunities that presented themselves, such as surfing. It was like an antidote for procrastination. Over 20 years I'd mentioned from time to time that I would love to try surfing, and I'd long envied the surfers I know, who are never less than totally passionate about their pursuit. On many occasions, I had been to places where it would have been ideal to learn but for whatever reason I hadn't. I don't exactly know why.

On the final day of free diving, we drove past an area that's renowned for surfing. I mentioned to one of the free diving instructors that I had always wanted to surf. He said he knew a good instructor and offered to bring me to the surf shop where they worked. Without a moment's hesitation, I said "yes." Would this have happened had I not spent the past week in nature and off my phone? Hard to say, but I definitely feel that being fully immersed (pun intended) in one water sport and out of touch with the rest of the world trained me to be more in the now, more connected with what was going on around me IRL in that beautiful part of the world.

If you unblock yourself in one area where you're procrastinating, it can have a snowball effect. If you prove to yourself you can do one thing, then you can easily do another because you're behaving as someone who does what they say and what they commit to. The more you do that, it becomes a sort of self-fulfilling prophecy. And staying off your phone is hugely helpful in that process.

But Remember to Love Thy Procrastinating Self

Many of us feel we will finally start to love ourselves once we have accomplished our goals—when we get that new job or promotion, when we move to a nicer house, when we tackle our bad habits, when we're no longer single. Often our self-love is conditional. We have a load of goals that we're not progressing on or anywhere near achieving. We're stuck, which feels deadening, but we also hate ourselves for being stuck, which compounds the pain.

I recently rediscovered a quote by Carl Rogers, the founder of person-centered therapy. It was a confirmation of what I see again and again in my work: "The curious paradox is that when I accept myself just as I am, then I can change." So true! It's only when we can like ourselves as we are—our procrastinating, phone-addicted, imperfect selves—that change can begin. We have to believe that we're worthy of the investment. If we're worthless, then what does it matter? Why should we try anything?

Emotional Freedom Technique (EFT)

For most of us, however, the process of beginning to like and accept ourselves just as we are is not so easy. One of the best tools I've come across as a practice in growing self-acceptance is emotional freedom technique (EFT), or tapping. Tapping is best described as an emotional version of acupuncture. It works by unblocking negative energy stored within our bodies, thoughts and ideas such as "I never get anything done" or "I leave everything 'til the last minute."

Take the first thought as the jump-off point for a tapping session. The statement you might work on would be "Even though I never get anything done, I love and accept myself completely as I am." You would then tap gently through key acupressure points in the body (illustrated below) while repeating some key words from this phrase (e.g., "never get anything done").

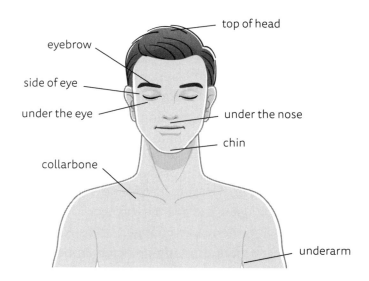

It seems counterintuitive to love ourselves for something which we may have lugged around with us our whole lives and centered our self-dissatisfaction on. However, what's really interesting is once we start up front with that, it creates space for other thoughts and ideas to emerge. If we can tell ourselves that's fine, we have that thing about ourselves but that we still like ourselves, it allows space for other possibilities to emerge.

I'll share one example of how I used tapping to good effect very recently. On the first day of my free diving course, a load of anxieties came up: "I'm not that athletic," "I haven't a clue what I'm doing," "Others know more." When I "tapped" on the belief "I haven't a clue what I'm doing," working through the acupuncture points shown in the diagram above, it gradually hit me: "No, I don't know what I'm doing, that's why I'm here. I'm here to learn." I reconnected with my original reason for taking this course—to learn something new! I could accept my fear as the whole raison d'être for the course. Sometimes an issue that initially seems very serious and complex can dissolve into laughter the more we bring the wisdom of both our mind and body to bear in relation to it.

Explaining the whole technique of tapping goes beyond the confines of this book, but it is relatively simple to learn and can be self-taught. EFT Universe (www.eftuniverse.com) is an excellent resource and offers some simple guidelines on how to get started. Alternatively, search for a tapping coach or therapist and work with them to show you the basic techniques. You can generally pick these up in a couple of sessions.

···················· **EXERCISES** ····················

Phone Usage Patterns (PUP)   **Week 6**

	Mon	Tue	Wed	Thu	Fri	Sat	Sun
Total estimated time							
Messaging, texting							
Calls							
Browsing							
Shopping							
Dating							
Facebook							
Instagram							
Twitter							
Porn							
Netflix, Amazon Prime, YouTube							
Gaming							
Other							

	Mon	Tue	Wed	Thu	Fri	Sat	Sun
Wait training: Note your phone-free activities or periods that you went without your phone.							

What were the feelings that came up today?

Monday:

Tuesday:

Wednesday:

Thursday:

Friday:

Saturday:

Sunday:

* * *

1. What did you try to reduce your phone use this week? Detail it here and rate its effectiveness on a scale of 0 to 10 (0 is totally useless, had no effect; 10 is totally effective).

_____

_____

_____

_____

_____

2. What can you do today?

Think about the number one thing that you feel you're stalling on right now. If you could just become unstuck and complete this particular task, it would have the biggest impact on your life.

Write it down here:

_____

_____

_____

_____

_____

Now, imagine how you would feel if in three months, six months, and one year you are still in the same situation, not having started on that task. When I ask my clients this question, they usually find that there's a set period of time they would feel okay with things continuing as they are, but that there is a definite limit to this.

For many the one-year mark seems significant. So when I ask, "This time next year would you still feel okay in this work/living/relationship situation?" They'll balk and say, "Absolutely not." When I ask them when they need to start getting the ball rolling to make their "within-one-year" time frame a reality, it will start to dawn on them how soon something needs to happen in order for them to achieve their goal within that period of time. Often, the answer is "pretty soon/now."

Write down your ultimate deadline for having your task completed:

_____

A key step in unblocking ourselves from achieving our goals is breaking them down into manageable steps. As the old saying goes, "a journey of a thousand miles starts with a single step."

In couples therapy I often get my couples to do a little visualization technique. It starts with them closing their eyes and slowly imagining symbols/images that represent the following: what their relationship feels like now, what they'd like it to be like, the obstacle that is blocking them from that improved relationship, what they need to overcome that obstacle, and then, finally, one that represents what they can do right away today to start making their desired vision a reality.

I encourage you to use the same visualization technique but substituting the "situation I'm unhappy with" for "relationship." This exercise works best after you've done some meditation first (see Exercise 4 on page 66).

Write or draw the symbols or words that came to you down here. Pay particular attention to what came up for what you can do today to enable your desired vision and commit to it!

_____

_____

_____

_____

_____

I'll be following up on this exercise at the end of the next chapter.

3. Knock stuff off the bottom of your to-do list.

Be honest with yourself. If you're never going to do that thing that you've been procrastinating over, that you really don't value, scratch it off your to-do list. To-do list items that we don't value, that we're never likely to do anyway, undermine our self-confidence. Remember, your time is limited! I scratched "sorting and compiling all my photos from phones, cameras, Google Images, WhatsApp, and CDs into chronological order on my computer" off my to-do list and it felt good! It's not to say I won't one day get around to that, but I admitted to myself that it was of low value to me compared to other, more valuable actions on my to-do list.

Stephen Covey's best seller *The 7 Habits of Highly Effective People* asserts that successful people are those who prioritize important tasks, regardless of whether they're urgent or not urgent. Covey classifies tasks along four lines: important and urgent, urgent but not important, important but not urgent, and not important and not urgent.

Unfortunately, many of us get stuck in the urgent but not important quadrant, what Covey describes as "frivolous distractions." He wrote his book in 1989, almost two decades pre-iPhone, and yes, even then people got distracted! I have no doubt that Covey would classify social media updates, email, and constantly checking the news as frivolous distractions. He asserted that too often we favor these over the not urgent but important stuff, such as updating a resume or pulling together a portfolio.

For me, the photos fell quite clearly in the not urgent and not important quadrant, so I scratched them off my to-do list after almost half a decade of languishing on it. Bring your attention to what's important for you by knocking stuff off the bottom of your to-do list. It not only clears up headspace but eliminates another piece of evidence in the case file of procrastination charges against you.

Complete this grid on page 102, making it as complete as you can. Take a good look at the not important quadrants, and be honest with yourself. Choose at least one item that has been hanging over you for at least a year that you have no desire to do and won't make a huge difference to your life anyway. Scratch it off. Do it now!

Important and urgent	Important, but not urgent
Urgent, but not important	Not important and not urgent

4. Proactive procrastination.

Anytime you have a big scary goal, one that might take a considerable amount of time, I encourage you to couple it with another one, preferably something completely different (e.g., decluttering the cupboard you dread opening). So when you feel like you're stuck on one goal, you can switch to the other one without feeling guilty. The minor task will help feed your belief that you can get stuff done. It's like a muscle, if we train this belief it helps build our confidence that we do what we say, even if it's just the minor things.

Ideally, the paired task will be something that you see value in quite quickly (to balance out the long-haul goal). While that wasn't the case with my gym work—sadly the muscle tone I was going for didn't just pop up during that one successful training session—the activity did give me a physical sense of well-being and helped bolster my confidence in tackling the writing goal. If you're not writing a book, your main goal could be updating your resume, putting together your portfolio—something that isn't necessarily urgent but is important in the long run. A less important task you could couple one of those with might be decluttering your wardrobe or finally working your way through your email backlog.

Pair two tasks below. Task 1 should be a big goal that might take some time to complete, and Task 2 a smaller goal you can see a return from more quickly.

Task 1

_____

_____

Task 2

_____

_____

CHAPTER 7

On Contentment

*"Happiness is when what you think, what you
say, and what you do are in harmony."*
—Gandhi

No matter what their presenting issue is, most of my clients will express in their initial email or during the first session that they would like to feel happier, more content in their lives. Hardly surprising, after all, the "pursuit of happiness" is even outlined in the Declaration of Independence as "an unalienable right," which is "given to all humans by their creator."

My happiness-seeking clients are typically looking for advice, pointers, maybe even short-cuts to that state which they desire. But what I've found in my own life and through my work is that the first step in becoming more content is getting to know ourselves. Unfortunately, this is something many of us shy away from as it inevitably involves looking at painful material, stuff we've suppressed because of shame or hurt.

Recently, while sitting in the sauna at my gym, I eavesdropped on what, to me at least, was a revealing conversation between two men. One was obviously following some particular program. Between precisely timed sessions of rather loud mindful breathing and less loud stretching, he would bolt out to the cold shower, grunt a couple of times in response to the icy water's impact on his body, then return, ostensibly reinvigorated, and repeat his routine. The other guy just sat there pretty quietly for the 15 minutes or so. They ended up talking about the infrared sauna and its benefits. The mindful breather asserted that "the only way to do it," if one wanted to get the full benefits, was to spend a certain amount of time in the cold water and a certain amount of time in the heat, and to do certain exercises alongside. He backed this up with an impressive amount of medical data and research. The other guy just nodded and said, "Yes, might be something in that." "Breather" wasn't quite satisfied with this response and was possibly a little irritated by the other guy's nonchalance and ease, which seemed to emanate from his every (thanks to the sauna) open pore, so said, "Well how do YOU do it? What do you think is the best technique?" His conversation companion just smiled and responded, "What works for me is what works for me. I stay here for as long as I feel my body is getting something from it." If you take one thing from this book, dear reader, I pray the "what works for me is what works for me" mantra is it!

One could probably divide the human race into two camps: the first is searching outside, looking for answers, proof, data (usually via a Google search), the other camp is just checking in with themselves, noticing what's making them tick and what does their body and mind good. Unfortunately, many of us have lost that ability to check in. We distract ourselves from the useful insights we get via our emotions and from what's going on in our bodies. We rely on the pacifier of the smartphone to defend against boredom or other unwanted emotions, putting off what's important to us while equally never letting ourselves switch off.

There is no recipe for happiness; it's a dish we need to devise from scratch to suit our own particular palate. Many of us are dutifully following hand-me-down recipes, passed from generation to generation, or we've reacted strongly against those recipes, ripped them up and focused exclusively on another completely different type of cuisine. But, unfortunately, that hasn't satisfied us either. In both cases, we're defining ourselves, our values, our tastes, in response to what we've inherited. There is no one dish that can bring happiness to everyone. But there are, however, certain basic ingredients in the "happiness dish" recipe that are essential no matter what your taste. And it's these I will focus my attention on in this chapter.

Healthy Body, Healthy Mind

According to the Buddha who lived around 2500 BC, "To keep the body in good health is a duty. Otherwise we shall not be able to keep our mind strong and clear." Roman poet Juvenal (late 100 to early 200 AD) concurred when he wrote *Mens sana in corpore sano*," or a "healthy mind in a healthy body."

The Romans and the Buddha were no slouches when it came to insight. They may have lacked precise scientific data, but they recognized one universal truth: Physical activity is vital for good mental and emotional health. I consider exercise a vital element to explore with any new client when assessing their overall level of well-being. If they're neglecting to do regular physical activity, I encourage them to reflect on the real reason for that. "Not enough time" invariably comes up, even though many of these clients may still manage to consume an entire TV series in one weekend! Nonetheless, almost each and every client will readily attest to feeling better when they do exercise regularly. Several consider their daily runs essential for their mental health and well-being.

If you take one thing from this book, dear reader, I pray the
"what works for me is what works for me" mantra is it!

My clients are not unique. In March 2018, the *Journal of Happiness Studies* published the results of an extensive review conducted by researchers at the University of Michigan on the link between working out and happiness. The researchers behind the study looked at 23 previously published works—15 observational studies and eight intervention studies since 1980—all of which found a clear beneficial relationship between physical activity and happiness. The number of participants in any one study was often small, but together, they represented more than 500,000 people ranging in age from adolescents to the very old and covering a broad range of ethnic and socioeconomic groups. Generally, the type of exercise did not matter, so long as the person was physically active.[53]

Exercise has also been shown to have a positive effect on addiction cravings. One study from Brown University published in the *JAMA Internal Medicine* journal, formerly the *Archives of Internal Medicine,* in 1999, found that women who engaged in vigorous exercise three times a week for 12 weeks were twice as likely to succeed in quitting smoking as women who did not.[54] Another, 2012 study published in *Psychopharmacology* found that smokers who exercised intensely for 10 minutes felt their cravings to smoke diminished.[55]

---

53   Z. Zhang and W. Chen, "A Systematic Review of the Relationship Between Physical Activity and Happiness," *Journal of Happiness Studies* (2018): 1–18, https://link.springer.com/article/10.1007/s10902-018-9976-0.

54   S. Turner, "Vigorous Exercise Helps Women Quit Smoking and Stay Smoke Free," *The Brown University News Bureau* (1999): 98–145, http://www.brown.edu/Administration/News_Bureau/1998-99/98-145.html.

55   K. Janse Van Rensburg, A. Taylor, A. Benattayallah, and T. Hodgson, "The Effects of Exercise on Cigarette Cravings and Brain Activation in Response to Smoking-Related Images," *Psychopharmacology* (Berl), vol. 221, no. 4, (2012): 659–66, doi: 10.1007/s00213-011-2610-z.

Unfortunately, despite their capacity to track our steps, link to other digital devices, and give us precise data on our physical activity, our smartphones are likely to make us more sedentary and less fit. A 2013 study of 300 college students by the College of Education, Health, and Human Services at Kent State University identified a negative relationship between cell phone use and cardio respiratory fitness. The researchers found that in comparison to low-frequency smartphone users, high-frequency users were more likely to forgo opportunities for physically active pursuits in favor of far more sedentary smartphone-based activities with a resultant negative impact on their weight and level of fitness. The researchers concluded that smartphones had a similar but even greater sedentary effect than TV and computers owing to the fact that they "fit in our pockets and purses and are with us wherever we go." Thus, they provide an ever-present invitation to "sit and play."[56]

Not only do our smartphones provide us with a sedentary "alternative" to exercise, but even when we do manage to get up and exercise, they can reduce the efficacy of our training.

I spoke to London-based personal trainer Matthew Galea-Naudi (@matthewgaleapt on Instagram), who works at White City House, part of the Soho House Group, and the Ritz Hotel, about the role of smartphones at the gym. Matthew explained:

> Ultimately, personal training is a "results" business, but often the real benefit I witness in my clients is the mental one—when clients really focus on just attuning to their bodies and allow that time for their busy minds to switch off. That can be just as powerful, if not more, than any muscle or aesthetic "improvement." Unfortunately, I'm noticing more and more clients being distracted by their phones at the gym, which means they're not fully focusing on what they're doing, failing to get the benefit from their workout, both physically and mentally. I've seen many gymgoers texting on cardio machines, which quite literally puts them off their stride. In addition, I've witnessed people receive anxiety-provoking personal or work calls halfway through their weight sets, which can trigger them into pushing themselves too hard, using poor technique when they feel riled up by what they've just been discussing. I encourage my clients to tune into their bodies completely, paying particular attention to the muscles they're engaging in any specific exercise. If they're

---

56   Lepp, et al., "The Relationship between Cell Phone Use, Physical and Sedentary Activity, and Cardiorespiratory Fitness in a Sample of US College Students."

distracted by their phone, they simply won't get the results they're looking for, and that's the best-case scenario. The worst is they injure themselves.

Research shows that we don't need to be marathon runners or gym bunnies in order to reap the health benefits of exercise. Relatively modest activity levels help us to maintain good health throughout life. The UK government recommends that over a week, activity should add up to at least 150 minutes (2½ hours) of moderate-intensity activity (e.g., brisk walking) in bouts of 10 minutes or more. One way to approach this is to do 30 minutes at least five days a week. Scientists have a good understanding of how regular exercise benefits organs such as the heart, muscles, and lungs, but they're now learning more about how exercise has a direct physiological effect on the brain, which impacts our mood and even our memory.

Dr. Áine Kelly, neuroscientist at Trinity College Dublin, researches the effects of exercise on the brain throughout the lifespan. She explains: "Research shows that being physically active throughout life, and especially early in life, can help to build resilience in the brain that protects its structure and function as we get older. We're beginning to understand more about the biological interaction between exercise and brain function that explains why exercise eases symptoms of anxiety and depression, and why those who are physically active regularly have a reduced risk of developing dementia in old age."

No Comparison

Comparing ourselves to others is one of the biggest threats to our well-being. Theodore Roosevelt nailed it when he wrote, "Comparison is the thief of joy." Whether it's our home, our job, our partner or lack of partner, our children or lack of children, or our level of core strength, it's a corrosive yet powerful drive for us to want to measure ourselves (sometimes literally!) against those around us. Comparing ourselves to others is, of course, nothing new, and most of us could easily cross-check ourselves either favorably or unfavorably against those around us even without ever having possessed a smartphone or social media account.

What social media has done, however, is broaden our scope for comparison. With the huge proliferation of social media and consequent widening of our frame of reference, it has become all too easy to compare our lot with that of our hundreds of Facebook "friends" and whomever else we choose to pit ourselves against—that blogger, that influencer, that celebrity, or that person we want to look like, sound like, or write like.

No longer confined to comparing ourselves to others, nostalgic features such as Facebook's On This Day feature actively encourage us to compare our current state to whatever state we were in at a certain point in the past. Can we really be living the moment if we're constantly referring back to past events? Why do we need to know what was happening "on this day" five years ago? There are so many ways this can make us feel unhappy. One is imagining you were happier then than you are now, which only serves to make you feel even more miserable in your present situation. Alternatively, if you see a picture that reminds you of a time you were very sad, rather than it triggering gratitude for being in a different situation now, it could perhaps awaken those old feelings. Either way, these memories serve to pull us away from the present, which is the only time we have any jurisdiction over.

A 2013 study by the psychology departments of the University of Michigan and KU Leuven, Belgium, on the impact of social media on young peoples' satisfaction with their own lives found that the more people used Facebook at one time period, the more their life satisfaction declined over time.[57] Another, more recent study by the University of Texas and the University of Georgia found that among 14- to 17-year-olds, high users of screens were more than twice as likely to ever have been diagnosed with depression or anxiety, consulted a mental health professional, or taken medication for a psychological or behavioral issue in the prior 12 months. Even moderate screen time was associated with lower psychological well-being.[58]

Constantly checking social media is like continually looking over our shoulder. It distracts us from what lies right under our noses, the things that we have power to change or to simply accept as they are. By focusing more on what's within our sphere of influence we can make better choices. The more we get caught in comparing, the less we're tuning into what makes us happy, what we can do to keep our side of the street in order. I'll often catch clients when they start to get blindsided by something they've seen on social media about an ex, a colleague, or former classmate. What's interesting is that they'll sometimes use criteria for comparison that they themselves don't even aspire to. At such times I will gently remind them that the "goals" they feel they're underperforming against aren't even their

---

goals! I'll encourage them to check in with their own personal goals and how they're doing in relation to those.

For instance, it might be that the client has been beating themselves up about the amazing promotion an ex-colleague got at a company they both used to work for but which my client decided to leave. In this case, I'll remind the client how they managed to achieve THEIR goal by finally take a leap of faith and exiting that well-paid job they'd felt miserable in. It's so easy to get distracted from our own lane and our own destination, the one that aligns with our own goals and values. Ask yourself, "Is this really my goal? Do I want the same thing?" when you feel like pitting yourself next to someone else's achievement.

Be the Change You Want to See

So many of my clients are frustrated with the world. It might be the state of the environment, wealth inequality, Brexit, the tragic Grenfell Tower or California fires, gender inequality, racism, or one of many other issues. What looms even larger, however, is their sense of frustration with themselves, with their feeling of powerlessness to affect change.

What I observe on Twitter, Facebook, Instagram, and in the comments section of many news sites is a great many people frittering away their energy, their power to affect change. Of course, many powerful movements have gained momentum on social media platforms before they take flight offline (e.g., #take3forthesea). But for each successful campaign, there are millions of others expressing their outrage or annoyance about something without being actively engaged in changing things offline. In a brilliant piece in *The Guardian* on in-group bias, Oliver Burkeman wrote: "Anger, stoked repeatedly over the long term with no tangible evidence that anything is improving, seems as likely to trigger 'learned helplessness'—the sense that whatever one does, the daily outrages will persist, making activism pointless."[59]

Many of my clients felt frustrated and angry about the Brexit referendum result and vented this frustration both on and offline. However, one of them did something different. Following several weeks glued to her phone in a social media bubble, reading and sharing material that just compounded her sense of anger and despair, she signed up to a political party, something she had never previously considered. She wanted to channel her

---

59   Oliver Burkeman, "The Vortex: Why We Are All to Blame for the Nightmare of Online Debate," *The Guardian*, November 30, 2017, https://www.theguardian.com/media/2017/nov/29/vortex-online-political-debate-arguments-trump-brexit.

frustration in a productive way. While Brexit was a done deal, she wanted to ensure that in the future she could get involved in campaigning on issues that were important to her. Another client who felt very distressed by the refugee crisis in Europe signed up to volunteer as an English teacher for refugee kids. Both felt an enormous relief to step out of their social media echo chambers. They no longer ranted online; instead they used their precious time, energy, and talents to take action and affect change.

What happens when we have strong principles, faith, or belief systems but don't act accordingly? Most of us feel immense frustration and anger. The biggest conflict I've seen in my clients is when they're living a life that is out of sync with their own principles. So even if it's expressed toward others—their family, partner, friends, colleagues, the government, those of opposing political views—that anger ultimately boomerangs back onto themselves. That's why Gandhi's quote on happiness at the beginning of this chapter resonates so strongly with me in terms of my client work. Our smartphones risk turning us into passive consumers, masquerading as activists, where to express our opinion on the latest shocking thing about <insert political figure that really riles you> is sufficient. We delude ourselves that we're engaging with the things that matter to us when we ensure that our family, Facebook friends, and Twitter followers know where we stand on certain issues. Except most of us are communicating to other people like us, in the same socioeconomic group of the same ethnicity, political persuasion, and religious belief/non-belief, whom we've self-selected as being sympathetic to our cause. If they aren't, well then with a quick click they can be purged or at least defriended. But talking into an echo chamber really doesn't satisfy for very long.

When working with a client who is particularly passionate on a certain issue yet not doing anything in practical terms to engage with it, I ask them what's stopping them. Often it's a sense of what they could potentially do just being a drop in the ocean. We really do underestimate our own power. It's worth remembering that a lot of seismic changes in society, like the abolition of slavery or the suffragette movement, were triggered by just a few passionate individuals. I'd also argue that even if, in the worst-case scenario, what you do seems futile and fails to spark a more communal effort, you will have gained a greater sense of contentment by acting in line with what you think and what you say. As Oliver Burkeman wrote in *The Guardian* shortly after the Brexit referendum: "The solution to feeling so despairing about the news, in short, is to let yourself feel despairing—and take action too."[60]

Know Thyself

Smartphones bombard us with data, news, entertainment, weather, and offers, but they don't tell us much about ourselves. I've had many a client who, in the wake of a bad breakup, googled for advice on how to get through it. They want to know how long it'll take them to recover, what's "normal," and what helps. These are not teenagers but rather educated men and women with challenging careers. While it's natural to want to avoid emotional pain and to look for a way out and reassurance that all is going to be okay, our phones can actively disempower us from figuring out what works for us, particularly when we're looking for answers to emotional questions.

If we are ever to learn how to heal our wounds and sooth our own distress, we first need to get to know ourselves. Most of this book has been focused on just that, clearing away the distractions from what you're really feeling, what you're avoiding, why you're procrastinating. Really getting to know oneself, or anyone else, takes time. And it takes compassion. How often have we given up on a friend or a lover because we find out something we don't like about them? We do the same with ourselves. The less we like ourselves, the less likely we'll want to explore who we really are. And sadly, the less we like ourselves the more we need to approach ourselves again with curiosity and care. If we don't know ourselves properly, it's like we're constantly off center, making decisions using other peoples' yardsticks, always turning to others (or Google) for advice, reassurance, and direction.

> *Smartphones bombard us with data, news, entertainment, weather, and offers, but they don't tell us much about ourselves.*

Most of the layers that obscure who we really are relate to things we've been told growing up, how we've been treated, and how we've adapted to that—either by rebelling or being "good and compliant." But you're not going to unearth your true self on your smartphone. Just as I'd recommend switching off your phone and spending time with your significant other to improve your relationship, you should do the same for your significant self!

---

60 Oliver Burkeman, "How to Stay Happy When the Sky Is Falling In," *The Guardian*, July 02, 2016, https://www.theguardian.com/lifeandstyle/2016/jul/02/how-to-be-happy-when-the-news-is-bad-brexit-trump-oliver-burkeman.

Disengage the drip feed of your smartphone and spend time in your own company. This can seem scary, particularly if you feel shame or feel unhappy with where you are in your life, but it is the only way through. As Big Sean once rapped, "if you love yourself, just know you'll never be alone."

When I work with clients I have the privilege to become acquainted with them over a period of time, usually upward of six months, and to witness their unfolding as they get to know themselves. Speaking to you via this book is never going to be the same. What I've tried to distill here are techniques to facilitate befriending yourself and discovering new ways of behaving that make you happier.

Even if you were my client, I could never possibly know you as well as you know yourself. Maybe none of the exercises speak to you particularly but my wish is that by reading this book you start to listen to yourself a bit more rather than automatically reaching for your phone whenever an uncomfortable emotion or thought comes up.

Ultimately, "what works for you" is what works for YOU. I recently met founder of Crystal Sound Lounge (crystalsoundlounge.com), Laura Franses, and we initially bonded over dogs. Laura told me that the only thing that worked to reduce her phone use was getting her dog. She had been monitoring her phone use for several months before she got her puppy, and although she was aware that she was spending way too much time on her device, she couldn't find a way to stay off it. When her dog arrived, though, her usage dropped by 66 percent without any conscious effort, and six months on, it remains low. Laura explains, "My dog compels me to be very present and engaged with what's happening in front of me, not what's happening on my device. An hour can pass in the park watching him bouncing around, enjoying nature and canine frolics without the urge for the addictive hit of the phone pickup."

There's a huge amount of research that illustrates that pet owners are happier and healthier than those who don't have pets. Dogs have been shown to have the most significant impact on our mental health and fitness. A report in the *Journal of Personality and Social Psychology*[61] based on three separate studies on the impact of dog ownership showed that dogs provide owners with "significant" benefits over non-owners. Dog people had greater self-esteem, better physical fitness, were less lonely, more conscientious, more socially outgoing, and had healthier relationship styles.

---

61   A. R. McConnell, et al., "Friends with Benefits: On the Positive Consequences of Pet Ownership," *Journal of Personality and Social Psychology*, Volume 101, Issue 6, (2011): 1239–1252, http://dx.doi.org/10.1037/a0024506.

Laura found that the dog was her thing that helped significantly reduce her phone time. But, of course, that's highly personal. For someone who is afraid of dogs, doesn't have an affinity for dogs, or is allergic to them, this example is probably not particularly relevant. But the point is that if you find something that matters to you, spending time on your phone will become less habitual.

Unlock Your Cage

Cast your mind back to Chapter 2, when I shared how the residents of Rat Park consumed less than a quarter of the cocaine-laced water those rats in solitary confinement did. I wonder how much less rats liberated from their cages would have consumed?

Most of us build and feather our own cages; we ourselves lock the doors and in some cases throw away the keys. We choose to confine ourselves in certain narrow spaces, thereby limiting our potential. When we're unsure of ourselves, we tend to find that confined space safer with its familiar routines and rituals. The more confident we start to feel the more we can try to explore new territory, venturing outside the cage of what we believe about ourselves.

Up to six months ago, if you had told me about your cat, I would probably have switched off. I would have been polite, tolerated the cat pictures, but inwardly I would have disengaged. However, when I started writing this book and in a bid to lower my phone use, I had to find new things to amuse myself with. During breaks in my working day, I'd sometimes go to the park (as alluded to in Chapter 4), but as I live in London, where it rains a lot, this wasn't always a possibility so I started to explore my place of work with new interest. The building is a bit of a labyrinth so it took various excursions. As I explored, I started forming a friendship with the resident cat, who is simply called "Cat." A beautifully plump, glossy-maned feline, "a circle with eyes"[62] who quite quickly learned how to ingratiate herself into my affections. This was major for me. I had identified as "NOT a cat person" for over three decades, and now here I was, reveling in my new feline companion. Even her name challenged me, as when I'd tell people about Cat and how fond I was of her, they'd sometimes assume I meant "cats." Initially I didn't (even though I loved Cat I wasn't prepared to tear up my identity as strictly and exclusively a dog lover), but she paved the way and now I really do love cats!

---

62   Catherine Gray, *The Unexpected Joy of Being Single* (London: Octopus, 2018).

I wouldn't have found this affinity for felines through watching cat videos on Instagram. In fact, Instagram probably has me encoded in some exclusively dog-obsessed algorithm. So my change of mind and heart could only happen IRL. Our phones limit us, serving us up more of the same based on past purchases, past likes, past news stories shared. However, some of my favorite books would never have been suggested through Amazon's incredibly intelligent "we think you might like" service. They just keep me with more of the same type of book, which, while enjoyable, doesn't really challenge me in the same way a new genre might. The books I've loved most have been ones I've found abandoned at a hotel or hostel when I've run out of reading material or grabbed hurriedly at the library when it's about to close.

But getting back to cats, you could say a love of cats is a pretty minor thing to discover about oneself. But even something so simple, so seemingly trivial as this limiting belief about my pet preferences did restrict me. Although I'm somewhat ashamed to admit it, in the past if someone said they had a cat as a pet, I tended to discount them as a potential close friend. We do this in so many ways, boxing ourselves off based on things we think we know about ourselves. We stick to people we know, interests we are familiar with, and defend ourselves from new thoughts, new ideas, new potential pets through the people/ media/organizations we follow, the apps we install.

This is most in evidence in the media we consume. Sixty-one percent of millennials use Facebook as their primary source for news about politics and government, according to a 2015 study by Pew Research.[63] As with Amazon, Facebook pages are personally tailored to our past likes and shares, making the political content we absorb a reflection of what we already believe so that it's just further entrenching us.

In what ways are you keeping yourself under lock and key?

---

63   Pew Research Center, "Millennial Facebook Users Most Likely to See Political Content on the Site," accessed January 12, 2019, http://www.journalism.org/2015/06/01/millennials-political-news/pj_15-06-01_millennialmedia10.

EXERCISES

Phone Usage Patterns (PUP)   Week 7

	Mon	Tue	Wed	Thu	Fri	Sat	Sun
Total estimated time							
Messaging, texting							
Calls							
Browsing							
Shopping							
Dating							
Facebook							
Instagram							
Twitter							
Porn							
Netflix, Amazon Prime, YouTube							
Gaming							
Other							

	Mon	Tue	Wed	Thu	Fri	Sat	Sun
Wait training: Note your phone-free activities or periods that you went without your phone.							

What were the feelings that came up today?

Monday: _____

_____

Tuesday: _____

_____

Wednesday: _____

_____

Thursday: _____

_____

Friday: _____

_____

Saturday: _____

_____

Sunday: _____

_____

* * *

1. What did you try to reduce your phone use this week? Detail it here and rate its effectiveness on a scale of 0 to 10 (0 is totally useless, had no effect; 10 is totally effective).

_____

_____

_____

_____

Retake the Smartphone Compulsion Test (see page 21). Has your score dropped?

_____

2. Food check-in.

In Chapter 2 I shared about the Rat Park experiment and its findings that "contented" rats are less likely to become addicted to cocaine even when it's freely available to them. Look back over the feelings you've noted down in the PUP charts. Are you beginning to see any correlation in terms of your smartphone usage and your mood?

Going back to the first chapter, one of the exercises asked you to think of your phone use as a food and what it would be. Take a moment and reflect, what would that food be based on your current use? Write it down here:

_____

Is there a difference? If so, what? Is the new food more appetizing, more nutritious, or just more satisfying?

_____

_____

_____

_____

_____

Also in the first chapter I challenged you to unsubscribe from draining/time-consuming group chats. If you did that, reflect on how you feel about what you've muted/unsubscribed from? Has it made a difference to your mood/energy levels/time?

_____

_____

_____

_____

_____

3. Find what works for you.

This exercise works best after meditation (see page 66). Close your eyes for a moment, take a few deep breaths, and ask yourself what will help you in particular switch off your phone more, to not be as dependent on your device. Write it down here:

_____

_____

_____

Now, get some Post-its and write down your personally tailored solution on them. Place them on your mirror, on the door of your bedroom, and where you usually charge your phone so you are exposed to your own personal anti-phone solution as frequently as possible. Now, compare it with the image you selected in Exercise 4 on page 16.

Is it the same? Maybe the first one is more inspirational and the second more practical. If they are two different things, take a photo of your Post-it message and use it as an alternate lock screen on your phone, or have one as your wallpaper and the other as your lock screen.

4. Find your happy.

Many of us are too busy, too goal-oriented to do things simply for fun, for the joy of the experience. This exercise is designed to get around those limiting beliefs and to encourage you to have fun again. It's adapted from Julia Cameron's *The Artists Way.*

List 25 things you enjoy doing, things that make you happy or have made you happy in the past. No matter if you haven't done them for years or decades, even if you're not sure whether you'd still enjoy those activities, just write them down anyway.

1. _____

2. _____

3. _____

4 _____

5. _____

6. _____

7. _____

8. _____

9. _____

10. _____

11. _____

12. _____

13. _____

14. _____

15. _____

16. _____

17. _____

18. _____

19. _____

20. _____

21. _____

22. _____

23. _____

24. _____

25. _____

Now, circle five things from the list above. Choose those activities that really appeal to you or that you're really curious about as to whether you might still enjoy them.

Choose one of these to commit to in the next week. As Julia Cameron writes, "Stop looking for big blocks of time when you will be free. Find small bits of time instead."

I will commit to:

_____

5. Live according to your values.

What fires you up? What most annoys you? What touches and affects you the most? Write the issue that springs to mind in response to these questions:

_____

It doesn't have to be a lofty purpose, it might not be about saving the world. Let's say your "thing" is dog poop on the street where you live. It really riles you. It's horrible to look at and puts you in a bad mood. Maybe you feel that it's inconsiderate of others not to pick up after their dog and is unhygienic, particularly for young kids who play in the area. Maybe you usually rant about that to your partner or on Facebook. While it may help temporarily to vent, in the long run it's not going to stop the problem.

Ask yourself what you could do instead. Could you write to your local council, ask them to put up signs about it? Report those who are breaking the law? If it's a political/governance issue, how can you get engaged? What would be the first step?

Now, write down what you're going to do about it In Real Life. What action can you commit to right now that might address your issue/cause, even if a small way?

_____

_____

_____

_____

6. Decouple happiness from success.

I did this by allowing myself to explore painting again with an attitude of play rather than accomplishment. Doing something we feel we're not naturally gifted at helps us to train our beginner's mind and is an antidote to perfectionism! It also helps us to break out of our boxes, to imagine a larger sense of possibility for ourselves, to create more options.

It's really good to be bad at something, yet give ourselves permission to enjoy it without judgment. If we can learn to allow ourselves to have this beginner's mind then our happiness becomes less conditional, less predicated on doing well, being recognized, and ticking off another accomplishment, whether it's climbing the highest mountain or running a marathon. Not to dismiss the merit of those activities, but if we can only be content within ourselves if we accomplish such things, then we will never know the joy of being still and present in the here and now, without lurching toward what's next.

Write something you've always wanted to try, if only you were brave enough/young enough/fit enough/talented enough. Can you permit yourself to try that thing, without judgment?

_____

_____

_____

_____

7. Procrastination recap.

I did warn you this was coming!

Refer back to Exercise 2 on page 99. What have you done in relation to that one thing you wanted to get moving on?

_____

_____

_____

_____

If you've started chipping away at it, well done. Keep at it!

If, on the other hand, you haven't yet taken that immediate first step toward doing The Thing You Really Need to Do, you're not a worse person because of that. The blocks in your way just require a bit more loosening.

Tapping/EFT, which I gave some guidance on in Chapter 6, is probably the quickest, most effective way to unblock. If you tried it and didn't quite get the hang of it, I strongly encourage you to try it again. If you didn't try it at all then you have nothing to lose!

If you haven't already done so, I'd encourage you to look through some of the videos shown on EFT Universe (www.eftuniverse.com/eft-resources/eft-tapping-tap-along-videos). Tapping along to someone else's issue, even if it's totally unrelated, while holding your own statement in mind, has been shown to be beneficial. This is a phenomenon called "Borrowing Benefits," which is based on the discovery that simply watching some-one else do EFT on their issues, while tapping along with them, can help you reduce the emotional intensity of your own issues.

Here are the instructions for Borrowing Benefits:

1. Pick an issue you'd like to work on. Write down a brief name for the issue in one to three words.

_____

2. Rate your degree of emotional distress on a scale from 0 to 10, with 0 being no intensity and 10 being the maximum intensity. Write down your number.

_____

3. Identify a part of your body in which you feel the sensation associated with that number, and write down the name of that particular body location.

_____

4. Recall an event in your life when you felt that feeling in your body. Pick the event that occurred the earliest in your life, if possible.

_____

5. Start tapping through the EFT points, as soon as the video session starts, and keep tap-ping 'til the end. When the person onscreen states their issue, state your issue instead.

6. When the video is done, think about the issue, tune into that same part of your body, and rate your degree of emotional distress a second time. Write down your new number.

_____

You'll usually find your number dropping substantially. If it doesn't, then pick another specific incident in your life most identified with that feeling in your body, and repeat the process. If you really feel you could do with more professional help, a face-to-face or Skype session with a tapping professional can be a very worthwhile investment.

Conclusion

"Take your life in your own hands, and what happens?
A terrible thing: no one to blame."

—Erica Jong

I recently watched a thought-provoking and somewhat disturbing talk by Brian Solis at the 2018 SXSW (South by Southwest) music and film festival and conference, on our relationship with technology. Solis is Principal Analyst and futurist at Altimeter, a company that provides research and advice on how to leverage disruptive technologies, and describes himself as having been a tech apologist in the past. In his presentation, he quoted Ramsay Brown, COO of Dopamine Labs, a company that develops and delivers an application programming interface (API) that enables developers to reinforce users for their applications (i.e., make their apps "stickier"): "We use AI and neuroscience to increase your usage, make apps more persuasive...It's not an accident. It's a conscious design decision. We're designing minds. The biggest tech companies in the world are always trying to figure out how to juice people."

Brown got a lot of flak after those comments were made public. I'd argue that the only difference between him and his counterparts among the West Coast tech giants and smaller start-ups who are focusing on app development is that he's uncensored and honest about what the end goal of his organization is.

In his SXSW speech, Brian Solis said, "If there's no leadership on the other side, then I think aside from selfies and fake news and bots that somebody has to take control, and I think that's just going to have to be you and me." He added, "Understanding your relationship with these devices, and not just your relationship with the device but the device's relationship with you...This has to change. It's not going to get any better. The technology that's going to be used against us...it's mind-blowing."

So what hope is there? The brightest minds and billions in venture capital funding appear to be directed at finding ways to hijack your attention, your mind, your wallet, your time. Meanwhile, regulation moves at a prehistoric speed next to the seeming light-year progression of AI, app development, and social media.

What defense does one person have in the face of this onslaught? In the Introduction, I mentioned that we have two powerful tools to defend against getting "juiced" (as Ramsay Brown described it) by the tech companies and whoever else is purveying their goods and services at us through the portal of our devices: our freedom of choice and our ability to change. These two qualities together have formed the cornerstone this book's narrative.

As writer Erica Jong said, "Take your life in your own hands." It's not the app or mobile developer's responsibility to look after you. But so often many of us wish that someone else would take care of us—our partner, our boss, our parents, our children, the government, regulators, teachers, etc., just so we don't have to do it ourselves, confront our demons, acknowledge what's serving us and what's not, and taking the necessary steps to safeguard our own selves.

Some years ago I used to frequent a yoga class on Thursday evenings in Soho, London. Invariably, on sunny evenings people would be milling about outside nearby pubs, laughing and talking loudly, the noise drifting into the open-windowed studio. Most of us got used to that but on one particular evening a nearby bar switched on some extremely loud bass-heavy music just as we were settling in to our end-of-class meditation. There were several audible sighs around the class and I myself thought that there was now no chance to have a restful meditation. The teacher, however, said something that's always stayed with me: "Be grateful for this because if you can meditate and find some stillness right here, right now with all this background noise, you'll be able to meditate anywhere."

Perhaps our phones provide the same challenge to us. If we can manage, despite all the alluring things our smartphones serve up to us, to still be attentive, to focus on the things that are important to us, to be fully present both to ourselves and our loved ones, but also have the capacity to switch off, then they truly can be tools that serve us rather than making us their slaves.

My hope, dear reader, is that you're finishing this book with a greater understanding of yourself, what makes you tick, what makes you click, and most importantly, what makes you content. I firmly believe that the more that you tap into the latter, the less time you'll spend swiping, clicking, and scrolling.

Appendix

Phone Usage Patterns (PUP)   **Week** _____

	Mon	Tue	Wed	Thu	Fri	Sat	Sun
Total estimated time							
Messaging, texting							
Calls							
Browsing							
Shopping							
Dating							
Facebook							
Instagram							
Twitter							
Porn							
Netflix, Amazon Prime, YouTube							
Gaming							
Other							

	Mon	Tue	Wed	Thu	Fri	Sat	Sun
Wait training: Note your phone-free activities or periods that you went without your phone.							

What were the feelings that came up today?

Monday: _____

_____

Tuesday: _____

_____

Wednesday: _____

_____

Thursday: _____

_____

Friday: _____

_____

Saturday: _____

_____

Sunday: _____

_____

Phone Usage Patterns (PUP)   Week _____

	Mon	Tue	Wed	Thu	Fri	Sat	Sun
Total estimated time							
Messaging, texting							
Calls							
Browsing							
Shopping							
Dating							
Facebook							
Instagram							
Twitter							
Porn							
Netflix, Amazon Prime, YouTube							
Gaming							
Other							

	Mon	Tue	Wed	Thu	Fri	Sat	Sun
Wait training: Note your phone-free activities or periods that you went without your phone.							

What were the feelings that came up today?

Monday: _____

_____

Tuesday: _____

_____

Wednesday: _____

_____

Thursday: _____

_____

Friday: _____

_____

Saturday: _____

_____

Sunday: _____

_____

Phone Usage Patterns (PUP)   **Week** _____

	Mon	Tue	Wed	Thu	Fri	Sat	Sun
Total estimated time							
Messaging, texting							
Calls							
Browsing							
Shopping							
Dating							
Facebook							
Instagram							
Twitter							
Porn							
Netflix, Amazon Prime, YouTube							
Gaming							
Other							

	Mon	Tue	Wed	Thu	Fri	Sat	Sun
Wait training: Note your phone-free activities or periods that you went without your phone.							

What were the feelings that came up today?

Monday: _____

_____

Tuesday: _____

_____

Wednesday: _____

_____

Thursday: _____

_____

Friday: _____

_____

Saturday: _____

_____

Sunday: _____

_____

Smartphone Compulsion Test

1. Do you find yourself spending more time on your cell or smartphone than you realize?	❏ YES	❏ NO
2. Do you find yourself mindlessly passing time on a regular basis by staring at your cell or smartphone?	❏ YES	❏ NO
3. Do you seem to lose track of time when on your cell or smartphone?	❏ YES	❏ NO
4. Do you find yourself spending more time texting, tweeting, or emailing as opposed to talking to people in person?	❏ YES	❏ NO
5. Has the amount of time you spend on your cell or smartphone been increasing?	❏ YES	❏ NO
6. Do you wish you could be a little less involved with your cell or smartphone?	❏ YES	❏ NO
7. Do you sleep with your cell or smartphone (turned on) under your pillow or next to your bed regularly?	❏ YES	❏ NO
8. Do you find yourself viewing and answering texts, tweets, and emails at all hours of the day and night—even when it means interrupting other things you are doing?	❏ YES	❏ NO
9. Do you text, email, tweet, or surf while driving or doing other similar activities that require your focused attention and concentration?	❏ YES	❏ NO
10. Do you feel your use of your cell or smartphone decreases your productivity at times?	❏ YES	❏ NO
11. Do you feel reluctant to be without your cell or smartphone, even for a short time?	❏ YES	❏ NO
12. Do you feel ill at ease or uncomfortable when you accidentally leave your smartphone in the car or at home, have no service, or have a broken phone?	❏ YES	❏ NO
13. When you eat meals, is your cell or smartphone always part of the table place setting?	❏ YES	❏ NO
14. When your cell or smartphone rings, beeps, or buzzes, do you feel an intense urge to check for texts, tweets, emails, updates, etc.?	❏ YES	❏ NO
15. Do you find yourself mindlessly checking your cell or smartphone many times a day, even when you know there is likely nothing new or important to see?	❏ YES	❏ NO

Recommended Reading and Resources

Books

Braza, Jerry. *Moment by Moment*. Boston, MA: Tuttle Publishing, 1997.

Cameron, Julia. *The Artist's Way*. New York: Jeremy P. Tarcher/Putnam, 1992.

Frankl, Viktor. *Man's Search for Meaning*. Vienna, Austria: Verlag fur Jugend und Volk, 1946.

Gray, Catherine. *The Unexpected Joy of Being Sober*. London, UK: Octopus Publishing, 2017.

Judkins, Rod. *Ideas Are Your Only Currency*. London, UK: Sceptre, 2017.

Levitin, Daniel. *The Organized Mind*. Boston, MA: Dutton, 2014.

Websites

The Center for Internet and Technology Addiction: virtual-addiction.com

EFT Universe: www.eftuniverse.com

Acknowledgments

Thank you to my commissioning editor, Casie Vogel, who placed enormous faith and trust in my ability to write this book. And to Catherine Gray (@theun expectedjoyof) who, as a highly successful published author, provided some really useful insights into the world of books and publishing.

To my beloved rescue greyhound, Madra, who is always by my side (when I have treats in my pocket) and my parents and siblings Jacinta, Lorna, and Ciaran, who instilled a love of books in me from a very young age, reading to me and making up stories for me.

To Dr. Áine Kelly for the brainy input, Nicola Joss for the well-being observations, and Matthew Galea-Naudi for the "fit bit."

Last but not least, thank you to my clients past and present who have taught me so much more than I have ever gleaned from books and lectures.

About the Author

Hilda Burke is an integrated psychotherapist, couples counselor, and life coach. She also holds the position of guest lecturer at the London College of Fashion, University of the Arts, London, and is a volunteer counselor at Wormwood Scrubs prison. Hilda trained as a transpersonal psychotherapist at CCPE, London, and holds a post-graduate certificate in dream work and couples counseling from the same institution. Hilda practices from her consulting room in West London, occasionally accompanied by the resident cat, or her dog, Madra.

Before qualifying as a psychotherapist, Hilda worked in PR, promoting many technology and telecom companies. She also trained as an actor.

Hilda's aim in working with clients is to help clear the obstacles to enable them to be able to listen to themselves, be true to themselves, and become fully authentic. She believes the ultimate goal of therapy is to facilitate clients to become their own therapist. Hilda is regularly called upon to comment on issues relating to well-being, relationships, and the challenges of modern life in the media and has been quoted in *The Daily Telegraph, The Guardian, The Sunday Times, The Financial Times, Forbes, The Huffington Post, Cosmopolitan, Psychologies,* and *Women's Health* and interviewed on the BBC, ITV, and London Live. In addition, she has contributed to three books: Lonely Planet's *100 Ways to Live Well* and the best-selling *The Unexpected Joy of Being Sober* and *The Unexpected Joy of Being Single.* She was a spokesperson for National Unplugged Day in 2016 and 2017. Follow her on Instagram at hilda_burke_psychotherapist.